995

UNSEEN KINGDOMS
By Bill Cox

This book contains over 60 photographs, drawings, charts and diagrams.

The author wishes to thank LIFE UNDERSTANDING FOUNDATION, Publisher of the PYRAMID GUIDE International Newsletter and friends, too numerous to mention here, for permission to reproduce many of the photos and illustrations featured in this book.

ISBN: 0938294-14-8

Published by:
INNER LIGHT PUBLICATIONS,
Box 753, New Brunswick, NJ 08903

The author may be reached at:
Box 30305,
Santa Barbara, CA 93130

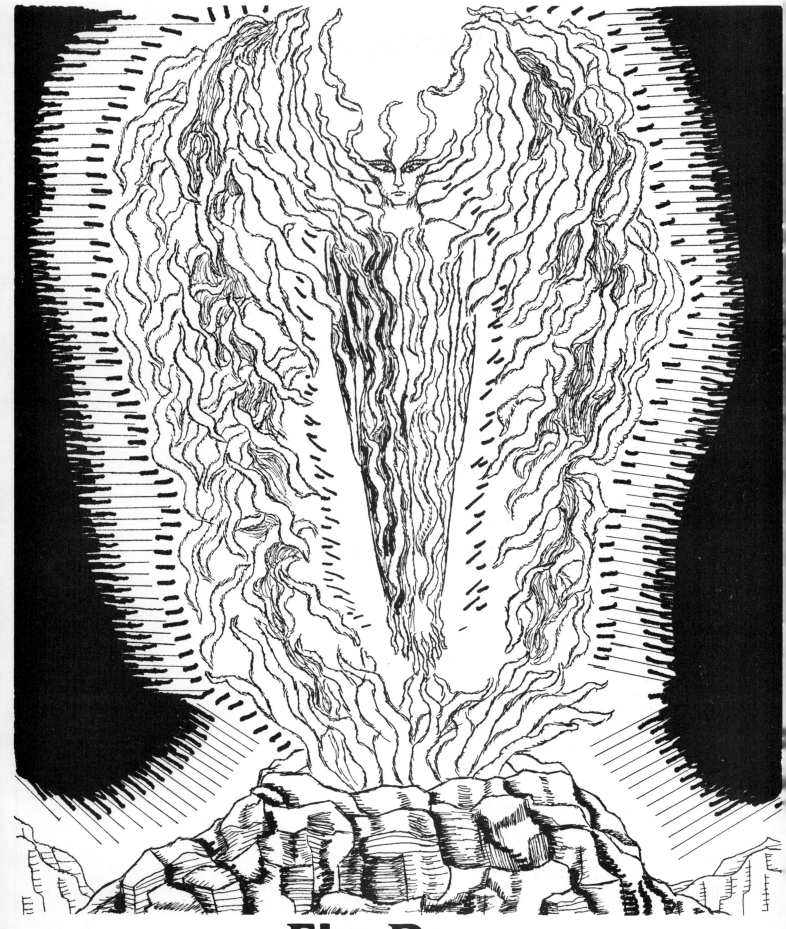

Fire Deva

Contents

Foreword

I came into this study about 15 years ago, not necessarily as a skeptic, but as one who really didn't know the meaning of the word psychic or other terms used by people investigating phenomena.

I once had one experience, which might have been a sighting, a UFO contact. I was coming back from Guadalajara, Mexico one night, in 1969, driving across the flat desert near El Centro, California, at about 11 p.m., when suddenly I saw up ahead to my right what looked like a welding torch. I watched this bright light with fascination because it became larger than any welding torch flare I had ever seen. It would first pulsate from brightness to dimness, ever becoming larger and brighter until it lit up the night sky like twilight. It lasted for about a minute reaching a maximum level, blinding my eyes before it pulsated down into a dim glow, then it held steady for a moment before completely vanishing. It looked like a globe, a London, England street lamp. After that event my life underwent many rapid changes.

In 1972 I began publishing the *Pyramid Guide*. The newsletter's main focus was in the realm of higher energies, exploring sources of free energy, anti-gravity, psychic phenomena such as dowsing, psychometry, mediumship, astral travel and so on. During the intervening 10 years, I received thousands of letters from all over the world telling of people having experiences that cannot be explained through ordinary physical scientific investigation.

We are dealing with unusual persons and events on a planetary scale, at an ever increasing and accelerated pace. It is becoming more commonplace to see humans demonstrate abilities, such as clairvoyance (extended sight), seeing lower into the spectrum (infra-red), or higher into the ultra-violet range. Some even go beyond into x-ray vision or night vision. A surprising number of people have acquired some degree of clairaudience. This means people can hear voices and sounds that are perceived from within and are little understood. The voice heard may offer guidance, issue a warning or may be a musical sound. Others develop clairsentience, the ability to feel something at a distance without touching it. I have personally been active in researching and writing about the phenomenon which also includes Dowsing and Geomancy. Although few humans know how to control and make positive use of these gifts, most can be trained to do so. But it requires time, self-discipline and infinite patience under the guidance of a noble and knowledgeable teacher.

Exciting research is going on in the world today with the use of biofeedback equipment, the electroencephalograph. By monitoring the brain waves of individuals, we are able to establish that there is some kind of electro chemical change going on in the brain of the person which can be scientifically recorded. Another important line of investigation is split-brain research. Science now knows a lot more about the mind and the brain than ever before. At last, the true value of intuitive cognition can no longer be ignored.

Through my own research, I've become convinced that the mind is apart from the brain. The brain is the computer center, the physical organ that receives, intellectually processes and sends the focussed information registering in our sensory apparatus and data from our intuition as well. Thus the mind is not solely the brain. The mind is a field of consciousness that interpenetrates the body and surrounds it. The mind can travel for great distances in an instant beyond the barriers of time and space, without limitations: to make contact with another mind, or another creature, object or substance in space.

Through split brain research we know that the right side of the brain directly serves the intuitive mind and is capable of perceiving objects in space outside the limitations of time. It can see at a distance, perceive and gather knowledge and information beyond that reported in the mind through the ordinary five senses. The left brain is also dominated by the clock-time world in which we live. It thrives on logic. Documented evidence now on hand, shows that the right brain can perceive and bring through data not ordinarily registering in the left hemisphere. The main goal of this research is the integration of the two hemispheres. This will happen between now and the end of the century, through new learning techniques working with the right side of one's brain, involving subliminal and superliminal perceptions. This information, no longer considered zany by progressive scientists, ironically has always been known by the world's great mystics for thousands of years.

What we need today is better equipment to prove that what we already know is intuitively true. Some work is being done in this area. Soon, we'll be hearing more about "subjective physics" and "intuitional instrumentation." These New Age Sciences will be greatly aided by sophisticated photography and better computer and electronic equipment, thus proving to the scientific community that it is possible to communicate with other dimensions and other realms of existence and verify the contact made with physical instruments.

Other relatively new—which are really rediscovered—sciences, include psychotronics and psionics (mind over matter) with or without the help of instrumentation respectively. All of the foregoing divisions of ancient and sacred sciences will be most useful in validating the true existence of UFOs and unseen kingdoms, or dimensions co-existing with our own planetary life systems, human, animal, plant or mineral.

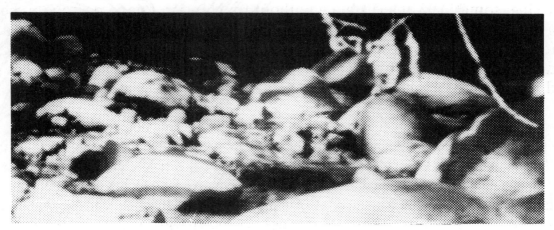

INDIAN SPIRIT PROFILE...upper right center of this unretouched photo, taken at a rocky stream bed by Rosella Roberts of Santa Barbara, California.

Air Deva

Elemental Forces and the Path of Evolution

At times, unseen forces such as color elementals, among those that make up the flowers, perfume essences, and so on, whose works we see in our gardens, are able to lower their vibration and manifest themselves physically, by grouping together as tiny invisible particles to form the petals. By fusing and injecting their bodies into substance as perfume of that flower, its color and ultimate geometrical shape, the whole flower is seen by us.

Generally speaking, these elemental forces are each made of one single substance, and they infuse that substance of their bodies into that which is to be made. For example, they are absorbed in the growing of a tree, into its roots, trunk and leaves. Uncountable elementals make up a single fruit blossom, or whatever. They combine with other elementals to make the physical form visible. Trillions of elementals are involved just in making up one blade of grass, coming in swarms from invisible realms, giving substance and energy to the form(s) being created. They implode themselves, drawn ever inward, sacrificing their bodies, infusing the essences of themselves. Color elementals come in and give up the exclusive atoms of their own existence, to give a blade of grass its greenness, its chlorophyll, and many other chemical elements that combine to give the grass blade its physical existence. It boggles the mind when one contemplates the numerical activity of elemental forces comprising a small lawn.

Since there are so many numbers and types of elementals, one can become confused in trying to magically communicate with a grass blade elemental, a daisy leaf elemental etc....What we see here is that a sub-microscopic entity is able to physically manifest in the visible world, under the guidance of some intelligence greater than itself; the Deva which directs its operation, which at a higher rate is broadcasting the essences of its own body, giving that substance to make some organic thing materialize in the physical world. We call this phenomenon "an act of Nature." The astounding thing about this activity is that these elementals seem to exist in a kind of plasma in space, which the occultists call the "ether." It is like an ocean, an ocean of finely attenuated air or water, and it contains, as I said, uncountable trillions of these tiny creatures in space, all waiting for the instance in which they are called upon to do the work they perform so well.

These elemental forces are on the path of involution, as opposed to man who is on the path of evolution. By that I mean that in his evolution man's duty is to grow and develop and improve himself with the power of mind, to better his environment. When he fails to do this he will die, or live contrary to divine laws. Man could reach immortality if he understood the true process of evolution and could carry it out to a perfect degree.

The involutionary forces, the elemental kingdom, these pre-physical creatures, instead of thinking their way through, operate by their feelings. So they experience great ecstasy when they give up their bodies or when they do what they are meant to do. They do not have the thinking mind to rebel against the guidance of the higher beings in their invisible realms of kingdoms. They do what they must do without complaint or resistance. It is their nature to obey, like we find in a colony of bees or ants. Besides, they would reject ecstasies awaiting their call, even if they could rebel.

The Devic beings directing these elementals are part of a hierarchy, and they are composed of more than one element. A simple elemental being is only composed of one element, maybe fire, and another consists only of water, whereas a composite being may be made up of two or more of the basic elements of earth, water, fire or air; and even of the element of the ether, which really constitutes a fifth class of this energy. There are other elements, of course, the elements of mind and emotion and of other things that we experience. The key is that there is a hierarchy, an angelic government that relates to all of this.

I remember a "Happening" in Santa Barbara, California. This was a celebration dedicated to the ecology of earth. An inner group got together and decided to invite the nature spirits to come. They meditated for a few days before the event, and invited the fire spirits, water, air and earth spirits, and any other entities of nature that might want to participate in the outdoor event.

On the appointed day, gas filled balloons were given out. I had never seen released balloons behave so strangely. Some went sidewise upward. There were also the fast climbers. Others stubbornly hovered in spite of air currents. Then, a most remarkable thing happened—dark clouds suddenly began to form in an otherwise clear sky and rain began to fall for a period lasting about ten minutes. Presently, the earth began to tremble, ever so gently, and lightning aroused by the storm started a mini forest fire nearby. So all nature spirits, at least, put in a cameo appearance in response to our invitation. Orthodox scientists would call it coincidence.

Perceptions and Electronic Recording— Tuning Into Other Dimensions

There are few people on earth who are born with, or attain a higher range of vision into the ultra-violet spectrum, beyond ordinary human vision, or below into infra red ranges which can only be seen with special lenses. Humans exist among us who also have infra and ultra vision; and one in 200,000 people are estimated to have night vision. So, here are some persons who have more evolved sight than others. This is also true of hearing. Certain individuals have super-audio perceptions. They naturally perceive audible sounds not usually heard by others. Some of these sounds are referred to as music of the spheres, or voices of the spheres, or messages from the spirit world. There are a substantial number of documented cases on record of persons seeing and hearing things invisible and inaudible to the average man.

The first time in my life that I saw an elemental force occurred in 1981, during a Frank Sinatra concert at the Albert Hall in London, England. There were thousands of people and an eighteen piece band. The forces really built up during the evening. I saw "sound elementals." They were coming from the orchestral instruments and moving around, experiencing their ecstasies as they changed speed, criss-crossed, altered direction and coalesced into new forms and colors before entering the ears and bodies of the listening audience. I can only describe the perceptions as being the result of combined visual inpicturing and outpicturing.

Cameras and recording equipment available to us today with the aid of the computer are scientifically qualifying this information, showing that it is true that there are things that exist in these higher and lower dimensions, energies which can be captured by photography or electronic recording equipment not visible or audible at the level of ordinary human senses.

If you are interested in working with the forces of mind energy, go outside on a cloudy day. Concentrate on changing the shape of a specific cloud. These tufts are so vaporous and easily dissolved with unblinking, focused eyes. This is one way of beginning psionic work; using mind energy to move or alter an object at a distance. With a camera, one must be quick; for as we know, it is only a matter of seconds before cloud-forms change or evaporate.

SEVEN PLANES OF OUR SOLAR SYSTEM	HIERARCHY OF UNSEEN KINGDOMS
1. DIVINE	GOD—LOGOS (Source of All)
2. MONADIC	PLANETARY SPIRITS
3. ATMIC	DEVA LORDS OF FIRE, FORM etc.
4. BUDDHIC	ADEPTS—AVATARS
5. MENTAL	ARCHANGELS, SOLAR ANGEL
6. ASTRAL	GREAT DEVA
7. ETHERIC (Pre-Physical Invisible	SUB-DEVAS
PHYSICAL (Visible)	NATURAL SPIRITS (Fairies, Gnomes, etc.)
	ELEMENTALS (Fire, Air, Water & Earth)

The Hierarchy of Nature and the Five Kingdoms

In the hierarchy of simple elementals, made up of one elemental substance, and the composite elementals, made up of two or more substances, there exists over them what are called Devas. The Devas are not always defined as conscious beings in human terms. There are two types of Devas described in the eastern world Indian teachings, the Rupa Deva and Arupa Deva. The Rupa Deva is usually perceived in human form…something like an angel. Arupa Devas are geometric in shape, or formless. Angels rule what is known as the fifth kingdom in the hierarchy. 1) Mineral, 2) Plant, 3) Animal, 4) Human, and 5) The Angelic.

Let's study the various realms for a moment. The first kingdom is made up of earth and solids, minerals and rocks. The second kingdom consists of plants and vegetation. The third kingdom contains the animal and creature world. The fourth division is humankind and the fifth kingdom reveals the abode of Arch angels, Devas, Nature Spirits (gnomes, fairies etc.) and the more simple entities known as Elementals of Earth, Undines (water), Sylphs (air), and Salamanders (fire).

The Devas actually draw their energies and life force directly from the Sun. Rupa and Arupa Devas thus function in the plane of lower Angels. They have this power to infuse a substance from their bodies into various elementals, each made up of a single basic ingredient we know as fie, air, water or of earth. This energy steps down in vibration until it becomes material or physical. It manifests on our planet as a plant, rock, an animal or as a human, or some part of them. They then become mixed combinations of minerals, vegetation, animal and so on. In this way, they produce certain forms, energies, structures, or foods, or whatever we need to experience life in the earthly realm.

Arupa Devas being non-physical entities, appear as geometric shapes or as formless substances. Some among them in lower vibrations are easily seen as clouds or smoke. They readily take on different forms, yet remain ethereal in their bodily appearance. This is not to say that an Arupa Deva couldn't become the spectre of a ghost, animal or a human, but basically, they are geometrically inclined or remain formless substance. A good example of an Arupa Deva is a snowflake. They say that of all the thousands, perhaps millions of snowflakes that have been examined under a microscope, no two are alike. Nor are two fingerprints identical. All are uniquely individual, yet remaining a part of the great Oneness. We can see also, the manifestation of an Arupa Deva in a crystal which always has six sides.

A growing quartz crystal invariably matures with 6 sides which may appear as unequal planes, but if you look closely, you can see six sides, no matter how small any one side may be; unless it has been damaged. This then would be either a natural quartz crystal, when it has just been found in a cave or in the ground, or one that has been grown from sodium or other elements in the laboratory. An invisible mathematical intelligence governs its form and growth. It is an Arupa Deva.

Whenever we see geometric shapes which are found throughout nature; pyramid forms, spheres, hemispheres, cylinders, etc...they are the product of Arupa Devas. Rupa Devas in human form are more inclined to work with higher life forms, especially Humankind. Sometimes, Arupa Devas reveal a detailed upper body, with the lower portion remaining less defined.

Above the Rupa and Arupa Devas then, are the Angels themselves. Archangels, being of the highest order, overshadow the different levels of lower Angels, Devas and unseen entities. This involves a whole pattern of study which I will not go into at this moment, except to allow for the fact that we are mostly dealing with the fifth kingdom predominately made up of involutionary forces. In the Fifth kingdom, however, there are evolutionary forces as well. These are thinking Angels, ones more concerned with great areas of landscape, or the movements of clouds, weather behavior, things our scientists refer to as geo-cosmic events. They are also concerned with volcanoes, earthquakes, floods, hurricanes; all kinds of earthly upheavals, including the more friendly types like rain, soft breezes, sunshine and so forth. They freely and intelligently work for harmony in the interaction of two or more elements and their behavior.

Visibility, Invisibility and Changes in Vibration

A striking comparison can be made between form units of etheric forces and UFOs. Either may suddenly become visible, and just as quickly fade away. Therefore, they are likely vibrating in an intermediate sphere bridging the prephysical (etheric) plane and the physical world in which we live.

Thus, it's conceivable that humans could travel in the ether if one could survive that state of vibration. An obviously gross person, however, might lose one's body during the rapid change from earthly existence into the finer frequencies of the ethers. But one doesn't have to leave our planet to succumb to humanly intolerable environments: sudden heat spells and freezing temperatures claim thousands of lives. Others are advised by doctors not to live in higher altitude, regions, etc....

In studying the electromagnetic spectrum we see slower vibrational energies are easily detectable through one's senses, without the help of instruments. A Sound Scale has been devised, denoting certain octaves, with touching registering at the lowest range. As the vibrations gradually speed up, we have sound. Going on up the scale we observe other ranges of energies ever increasing in frequency.

PART SCALE OF COSMIC OCTAVES & VIBRATIONS (approximate)

TYPE OF ENERGY	OCTAVES	VIBRATIONS PER SECOND	
COSMIC	62-	4,611,686,018,427,387,904 to	?
Gamma Rays	62-80+	4,611,686,018,427,387,904 to	?
Psychic Proj.	60-80+	1,152,921,504,606,846,976 to	?
X-Rays	56-61	72,057,594,037,927,936 to	4,611 x
Spirit Electrons	51-57	2,251,799,813,685,248 to	144 x
Perfumes	51-57	2,251,799,813,685,248 to	144 x
Ultra Violet	51-56	2,251,799,813,685,248 to	72 x
Chemical Rays	50	1,125,899,906,842,625	
Solar Color Spec.	48-57	281,474,976,710,656 to	144 x
Visible Light			
Physical Color	48-50	281,474,976,710,656 to	1,125 x
Heat	46-48	70,368,744,177,644 to	281 *
Infrared	38-48	274,877,906,944 to	281 *
Electromagnetic			
Microwave	28-38	268,435,456 to	549 #
Electricity	25-35	33,554,432 to	34 #
Electromagnetic			
Longwave (Radio)	14-29	16,384 to	536 γ
Physical Sound	4-15	16 to	32,768
Touch	1-4	2 to	16

* add twelve decimals — x add 15 decimals — # add 9 & γ add six.

Alexander Graham Bell was once quoted in a scientific magazine article published some eighty years ago, in which he said, "If you place a rod in the ground and electrically vibrated this rod, at first you would feel its oscillation. If it were vibrating a little faster you would expect to hear a hum coming from the shaft. Should it be heightened further, it would eventually become magnetic. By adding more resonance to the rod, it would begin to produce electrical energies. Further increasing the rod's intensity, would then cause it to become warm, proceeding onward through the temperature range, revealing colors associated with heat; red, orange, yellow, blue, violet and so on. Then, as the vibrations are augmented, it enters the radio spectrum, producing radio waves. Beyond that, it would enter the chemical range in the forty-eighth or forty-ninth octave. Still increasing the intensity of oscillation, it will begin to produce light around the fiftieth octave. A little higher up it goes into the realm of x-rays. Here, it would become dangerous to touch, or to be too near the rod. More rapid oscillations cause the rod to give off gamma rays—very dangerous to the human form. Then proceeding on up higher in the spectrum, the so-called cosmic rays begin to make their presence known. So from a few vibrations a second, to countless millions (numbers with seventeen or eighteen decimals) the rod continues to blur as it vibrates with increasing intensity. Eventually, it will become invisible, and then who knows where it would go from there."

I believe this is what happens to UFOs. The controlling operator changes the craft's vibratory levels, according to the need of the moment. Both UFO and operator—if he's aboard—change in substance, and thus have this great maneuverability and capability to disappear in the sky, a phenomenon observed by so many credible witnesses since 1947.

Extraterrestrial, interdimensional and thought-form entities are conceivably of a more advanced evolutionary development, enabling them to withstand these sudden changes in vibration. Unless the life giving frequencies were harmoniously stabilized for human occupation within a moving UFO, I seriously doubt if an ordinary mortal could survive the experience.

Plant Deva

UFOs and Unseen Kingdoms

CREATING AN ARCHETYPICAL FORM AND BRINGING IT INTO MANIFESTATION

Because so many UFOs are of geometric design being disc, round, cylindrical or cigar-shaped etc., these craft are in reality materialized thought forms. UFOs have been originally created in the invisible planes as a result of the thinking of men existing somewhere. Because of this fact, whether these spaceships are considered to be wholly material or not, they have in the past been conceived and developed in the minds of intelligent beings.

A master archetypal plane exists in the lower mental plane. It also functions in the higher mental world, depending on the quality of the form in which the thought occurs. It is like an invention. If someone devises a new idea for a product and creates intense thought power, putting a lot of focused energy into it, pretty soon the invention is going to manifest in our material world. It may take physical labor and materials to do it, but it will likely appear as a result of the accumulation of thought forms driven by the will of man.

Thus the form archetype is created in a thought form, desire world through the medium of focussed mental energy. It is in a highly attenuated state in this thought form plane, not yet containing much organized substance. As the will for the form to manifest is felt on the various planes, it lowers in vibration from higher mental spheres. Then, the thought form taking shape —in the process of becoming—descends into the lower mental realm, where it might acquire certain scientific qualities. Finally, the finished archetypal form truly exists yet cannot be seen in the physical world. This is the portal, pre-physical stage prior to actual transduction, so that it may be perceived by human senses.

As a person brings in emotional energy—being really enthused and wanting the desired idea to manifest—emotional energy then helps to bring the archetypal form down in vibration. A copy of the archetypal form now exists in the emotional plane (Astral). From the emotional plane—as the person really pictures the thing inwardly—it begins to acquire subtle energies in the etheric realm necessary to bring the form into worldly existence.

This great ocean of energy known as the ether is the prephysical state, where the invisible mould holds the atoms of the material form together. This is where the invisible composite elemental forces are often instantly summoned to join together in bringing the material invention into being, where it can be seen and felt as solid, and semi-solid form for use in our structured world. Of course if the materials have already been mined or harvested, man and machine begin to give the form(s) their physical identity for use in our world.

In consideration of the foregoing analysis—based upon secret teachings of the ages—some UFOs sightings, where witnesses are confronted with the "Now you see them....Now you don't" mystery, these reports may at least be explained with some justification. I don't, however, believe that *all* UFO thought form ideas we may see entering our atmosphere are likely the product of humankind living on this planet. The next step in pursuing this line of investigation, is to find rational explanations as to why any interdimensional or extraterrestrial entity should conceive such thought forms in the first place…and to what earthly or unearthly purpose these spacecraft may serve?

UFOs Thought Forms, Ours or Theirs?

On a higher level, the potential exists, that if a person could conceive of, and dynamically hold focus on the invention, from beginning to end, one would not have to go out and gather the materials. One would actually be able to think the form idea into being. Most humans can dissolve a cloud with intense mental focus, but to create a cloud-form in a clear sky is another matter.

Few people on the planet today have the power to create a thought form (whatever their need may be) and have it manifest in the physical. However, we have heard such things as bi-location, where a person can be seen in two places at once, materializing an astral counterpart of their physical body. Certain yogis in India can send their astral body out and gather material substance to it so that they can be photographed occupying two places at the same time. According to the "law of apports" a person can make an object disappear and then reappear at another location, impelling the object through space by desire, working with the elemental forces. Feats of this type are not subject to the limits of time and space as we generally consider them.

So, if UFOs can be the result of thought forms, either the need is there by beings more evolved than we are—of whom we may or may not be aware and of what these needs actually are—or they may be the result of an accumulation of thought forms generated by people living in different parts of the world, perhaps spanning long periods of time. Hence thought forms given sufficient energy and focus could start the form idea vibrating in the archetypal sphere of the mental form plane. As desires intensify and multiply, through repetitious persistence and the wills of scheming, thinking people, the energies coalesce, gather power, and according to their focussed intensity, begin vibrating down through the invisible planes. The composite idea vector sometimes reaches our physical plane.

These thought forms are more often than not energized by Arupa Devas. These form building creatures, with others that infuse the object with the substance of their own bodies, make up the disk, sphere or cigar-shaped object; whatever it may be that we label as being a UFO flying through space.

Why do UFOs so commonly appear in the foregoing described shapes? Is it because that is the way we humans subconsciously want them to materialize? Perhaps UFOs are the forerunners of earthly spacecraft which will one day provide our future means of travel? Are we seeing craft by means of premonition, vehicles which are already functioning on the inner planes, awaiting that precise moment in time for them to serve humanity in our physical world? Maybe they are entirely practical in the finer spheres of existence, but many types of UFOs are simply unable to maneuver and stay aloft for any given time in our global atmosphere. Therefore, thought form craft from the invisible realms may possibly burn-out, dissolve or quickly change vibration in order to survive and safely return to etheric astral or mental planes from which they came.

On the other hand, if they were solely the works of geometric, Arupa Devas then their origin and purpose would have to be studied and considered in different terms. In this case, the would-be, strictly extraterrestrials, as we think of them, are rather interdimensional in origin. And we have the "anachronism," a kind of Fortean person, place or thing existing out of its time—past or future. Buggy whips and mustache cups in their day were in great demand, now these items are treated as a novelty, having generally outlived their usefulness. Are UFOs anachronisms reintroduced from an advanced past or future?

Sounds of Power— The Modern Alchemical Laboratory

Another aspect of this phenomenon is, that if we are working with pre-physical energy—forcefields as mysterious and effective as those used in spiritual healings—then elemental forces can be summoned, if the energized thought form is strong enough. This power that makes it possible for tiny, invisible entities to congregate and materialize, even in a pre-physical state, is done with the power of thought and a word, or a sound of power.

Sound is a very potent energy, which in terms of UFO investigation, needs more open minded study. Today, in a laboratory, with ultra-sound we can literally dissolve materials, even stones and hard objects in moments, literally vaporizing them. So we are already scientifically able to destroy various types of forms. They visibly cease to exist. Building up forms and preserving them usually requires different skills and consumes longer periods of time.

The difficulty is in creating. Science is, however, commercially synthesizing rubies, diamonds, emeralds and other stones in the laboratory. They are now made with such high quality that is is very hard for even an expert to tell a synthetic stone from the real thing. In appearance the untrained eye only sees a kind of sameness, we must remember though, that this time of creativity requires physical components at the start.

The only thing that determines the difference is the price. One could spend thousands of dollars for a tiny ruby and maybe only a hundred dollars for a synthesized one, even though they are of the same shape and color. Value is set by the fact that one is synthetic and not created by nature, while the other one is of a very high order of vibration. Whether made by man of nature, both owe their continued existence to an ongoing, master form sounding its key note in the archetypal spheres. As long as that archetype exists, the form will continue to exist. Finally, when the archetype or material form is destroyed, or has at last decayed beyond recognition in the physical world, all form, life and pattern integrity vanishes.

Healing Elementals From the Unseen

ODILON STUDIES X-RAY…prior to doing the healing work.

A mysterious invisible healing process goes on when we cut our finger. A scab forms and then it may or may not develop a scar. We call this force "Nature" and we take it for granted. It happens in an intelligent fashion and can be delayed according to the health of the person or negligent care that one gives to the wound. On the other hand, there are numerous documented cases of immediate or accelerated healings on record.

On two occasions in Brazil, I personally witnessed immediate chemicalizations, healings that were supposed to take place over weeks and months, or even years. There were cases in which doctors said that no total healing was possible and where the usual methods of drugs, treatment through radiation, therapies, etc., had failed. These were patients confronted with the prospect of dying, or at least losing the offending organ or limb through surgery. So in desperation, they looked for a cure through other (metaphysical) means.

I've seen this in my investigations of Odilon, in Brazil, whom I wrote about in an early edition of *UFO Review*. Odilon has shown how new bone and tissue can be grown in seconds. Therefore, he is using the powers of these elemental forces. Perhaps he is not doing this directly. He feels he is working with certain entities whom he can see and speak with, while others cannot. We have tried to photograph these specific entities but have been unable to do so. But, Odilon and others with similar powers can apparently see them. However, photos of similar energy bodies recently appeared in a past edition of *UFO Review*, in my article entitled, "Spacemen, Show Us Your Powers."

Elementals are the healing spirits that begin the process. These elementals are there when you cut your finger. It doesn't matter if you are in the U.S. or in Arabia. They are instantly drawn to your wound because of the ecstasy they experience when fusing the substance of their own bodies into the damaged tissue to bring about the healing. They are as quickly attracted to the scent of blood in the air, as are ravenous sharks to a bleeding body in the sea.

Angels working with growth, repair and preservation must have an environment that is attractive to them or they will depart. Imagine a group of little healing angels, flying around a person while emanating their lovely fragrances, tinkling their music and radiating joy, when suddenly the person becomes verbally abusive. They are going to fly away, just as we would depart from a party where someone was misbehaving. So, the healing angel will bring in positive energies to the one who needs them, if the one so afflicted and the healer provide the ideal healing environment. Some people defy the "getting-well" process by eating wrong or thinking wrong, or whatever, so that the healing angel's essences cannot work at a maximum level. Rest, relaxation and sleep seem to provide the best healing frequencies. Here, the etheric (vital, pre-physical) body seems to regenerate itself through calmness, rest and sleep.

Certain prephysical entities can be seen, felt and controlled by people who understand the nature of the laws under which they operate and are governed. These laws enable all elemental forces to work totally in the invisible world, unseen by humankind in general. Fortunately, seen or unseen, controlled or uncontrolled, they go on doing their "good works," exacting no repayment, unless we interfere with the healing process.

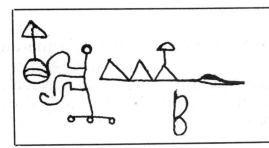

CARTOON-LIKE, EXTRATERRESTRIAL INSCRIPTIONS... sketched from an illustration reportedly obtained from R.P. Reyna. The figures appear to represent two airborne or anti-gravity powered craft with occupants happily cruising along. But Wait! This illustration has been purposely placed upside down to demonstrate that it is more comprehensible inverted than in its upright position. Recent and meticulous inspection of Egyptian, Mayan, Sumerian and other ancient glyphs, pictographs and related symbols and drawing often reveal upside-down figures. These cryptic emplants served a noble purpose,

The Builders, Preservers and Destroyers

As we know in nature there are three basic types of elemental forces—and this may be an oversimplification. 1) The builders. 2) The preservers. 3) The destroyers.

Everything has a decay rate. In fact, science uses this method to determine the age of ancient artifacts and objects, stones and so on, by using a carbon radiation, decay method. Science does this by judging the normal decay rate of an object and then estimating its age. Moreover, we have quick decay foods such as apricots, bananas and peaches. After a few hot summer days they will decay very quickly. If you leave an egg out of the refrigerator for very long it will soon rot. With some objects or substances such as metal, the decay make take thousands of years. Nevertheless, everything—even metal—must go back to its source. In the laboratory they talk about isotopes and radioactive substances. The isotope's half-life may be one thousand years, still the isotope and all unpreserved things are in various rates and states of decay.

With the builders we see new plants and flowers coming out of the ground. New cells form in our body and so on. We have this growth and building process going on among the elemental forces wherever life exists. A kind of ever changing, life renewal process can be seen all throughout the human and subhuman kingdoms.

When we learn to work with the preserving forces, we can prolong our life. We are able to stay healthier. Lower temperatures will slow down the decay rate of bananas and peaches and apricots. We have found that the pyramid will do this, just the pyramid form will do it. We must remember that the destroyers are not bad because they destroy. They are only doing what they are supposed to do. We are continually having this building up, preservation, and breaking down of all material things so that new ones can come in and take their place. That is the function of evolution and involution, and it will go on as long as earth exists.

Life Isn't Easy for Space Emissaries

There are emissaries among us who know who they are, and even remember their race or culture of origin. They also know the star system or galaxy or constellation they hail from. They instinctively know this from the time they are born. Most are sworn to secrecy. It would be to their disadvantage to reveal the nature of their assignment. Some are involved in politics, science or religious work. Others whom we consider to be geniuses, giants in their field, charismatic leaders, master teachers, the wise ones, among them will be found the true emissaries.

Water Devas

Various emissaries only have a vague idea of who they are. They know they are quite different from average man. They may even be misfits in the physical world. Being the unique persons they are, emissaries may often be considered "out of step" with society. It would be the same for us, if we had to go down a notch from where we are on the evolutionary ladder today and live with a civilization of savages. We would have to make changes and downward adaptations.

For many advanced entities, consciousness and memory is veiled, because it could be to their advantage not to remember from where they come. Otherwise, it could be too difficult for them to cope with life in this world. They only know that they are here because they have a special assignment. Not carrying out this duty would be too devastating, so they must succeed. A few here and there are figuratively going crazy trying to understand what the yet unknown assignment may be, so impatience often leads to escape, excesses and failure.

I find that among this group, some become excessively involved with alcohol, drugs and sex, or maybe athletics; anything to try to mentally escape from this—our world. Several knowingly, or instinctively, want to get back to where they came from. So, they look to alcohol or whatever. These people really need help, but it's not likely that they will find it from people who are closed in their opinions about UFOs, and things not of this world.

All too often, these veiled emissaries may have mental, emotional and sometimes physical problems, so great understanding, patience and empathy is required. Self-delusion, an egotistical attitude of self importance, or the opposite extreme, low self-esteem, are often signs to watch for.

Why should the change from one planetary life system to another be so traumatic? Suppose there is no war, sickness or death where they came from. Perhaps their food and drink was made up of purse essences, even quintessences. Maybe their social and family life was for the most part harmonious. Imagine then, what a comedown one would find upon awakening into our earth life. The adjustments would be horrific. Unable to cope with the new environment, it's conceivable that the entity could become neurotic and seek the most readily available escape routes at hand. Neurotic and addicted, or seemingly eccentric persons aren't necessarily ignorant. To the contrary, most are very intelligent and gifted human beings.

Edi's Special Mission

Edi, in South America, is about thirty years old. She has known all of her life that she has a special mission to carry out on earth, though the details of that assignment are not yet entirely clear to her. She is an accountant for a major industry in Bolivia. Because of her extraordinary gift to work with math and numbers, Edi feels certain that her ultimate mission will be

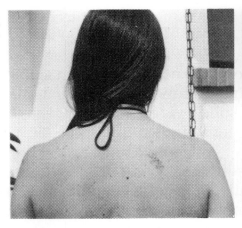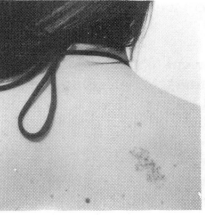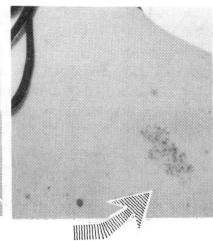

EDI'S BIRTHMARK...of an unnamed constellation in the cosmos.

focussed along this line. Moreover, a New York astronomer, and personal friend, who studied the patterns in a birthmark on her back, believes that the configuration closely matches that of a major constellation in space.

Years ago, Edi was approached on the street by a man who was perhaps in his fifties, with white hair and a white beard. He called out to her from behind saying, "Edi, you are one of us...you have the birthmark on your back." She had never seen the man before, and she was not wearing a low-cut dress, so that the birthmark could be seen. "I'm going to give you this book," he said, reaching out to her as she turned around to see who was speaking to her. "Keep it as long as you want. It contains the information you need because your work begins as of now." (The man in this case is considered to be a messenger.) He told her that he was from the same constellation and showed her a birthmark on his arm that clearly matched her own natal blemish.

So Edi took the book home and read it. Then she reread it, only finding information which she thought was interesting, but nothing outstanding. Not having seen anything special about it, she kept the book for about a year and a half. Meanwhile, the book sat on the shelf all of this time unnoticed, and she had completely forgotten about the incident.

Then one day Edi pulled the book down off the shelf and began to read it. On the first page she got the message; for the first time in her life she knew what she had to do. A few weeks later, and on impulse, she put the book in her purse and went out. Presently upon leaving work to go to her car Edi heard a voice say, "Thank you for returning the book." It was the same bearded, white-haired man. How could he have known, unless it was through telepathy? She returned the book and his last words were, "You will be contacted again soon."

Several months later Edi was eating dinner by herself in a La Paz, Bolivia hotel She had been sent to La Paz to do some work for her out-of-town employer. Presently, a man about 6'7" tall approached her. He said, "Edi, I am glad to see you here. May I sit down? I know about your birthmark. I also have one." Her first reaction was to say no to a total stranger, but she felt he was sincere. Then he said, "I don't want you to think that I wish to invade your mind, but I read your thoughts, and it's O.K. Am I not correct?" Then, before Edi could reply, he quickly sat down and rolled up his sleeve, revealing the same birthmark on the inside of his left forearm. For the sake of convenience, we shall call this blond, fair-skinned and rather handsome man "M."

The next day Edi and "M" went to an ancient site in Bolivia, known as Tihuanacu. It isn't what the archeologists are claiming it to be. It is an ancient Initiatic and Sacred Ceremonial city ruins of puzzling archeological interest. If we'll ever find solid evidence that ancient Astronauts ever visited our planet, Tihuanacu is a prime location for investigation.

Anyway Edi asked "M" for proof that he was sent by a higher power or intelligence and would he demonstrate some unearthly capability. Apparently, the man levitated his body and also levitated a very large stone. "M" said, "Edi, you must now learn the power of your mind. I want you to mentally raise the stone." Edi threw her hands up and replied, "But I can't levitate things." "M" said, "Yes, you can." He again levitated the stone and after a time, Edi said she managed to hold it up, although it was wobbling and sinking slowly back to the ground. Then "M" added, "That's a good first effort." Although Edi couldn't mentally raise the stone from the ground–up, she said she was able to momentarily hold it in space with his help. "You'll gradually learn to do it by yourself." Then he led her through the ruins of Tihuanacu, detailing the history of their forefathers who came there from space in the dim, distant past.

She was contacted later in Miami by a young man from Chile, who also had the same birthmark. He gave Edi another message of what she was to do. As I recall, she said his marking was located on his right hip. Before I left Bolivia Edi took a group of us British and American researchers to Samaipata, a place which was about 120 kilometers west of Santa Cruz, Bolivia. It is also one of the world's most ancient and enigmatic sites. No one I ever heard of has the slightest notion of what this carved out, red sandstone hilltop is all about. One thing is sure, the ancient engineers and sculptors worked with elemental forces every step of the way, from planning to completion. Samaipata could well have been an ancient landing and launching site for extraterrestrial craft. This possible explanation merits just as much investigation as any of the leading but implausible theories advanced by archeologists familiar with the site.

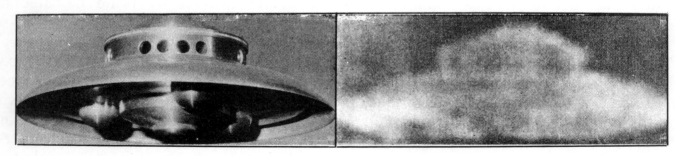

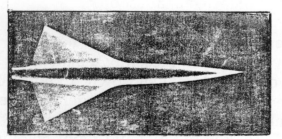

THE CLEAR UFO IMAGE...(upper left) may—abruptly or gradually fade away into oblivion (right) or vice versa. At what speed would the rocket (left) reach the range of invisibility?

POLAROID PHOTO SEQUENCE...all taken consecutively, within a few minutes of each other. Frame 1. Bill Cox and Mauro Pinhiero pose. Frame 2. Paul takes Mauro's place—picture takes on more light. Frame 3. Light increasing, yours truly beginning to fade, Paul remains clear. Frame 4. Background almost unrecognizable. Paul still clear, but I'm even more undefinable.

Photographing the Spaceman: To Appear or Not to Appear

Paul, a South American spaceman gathers unusual data and he is setting up a research center near Brasilia, Brazil. Like most of the space people I met, he is financially secure, but not for the sake of money. Paul isn't chasing after material things. His main goal is to serve humanity. He gives a lot and has noticeably subdued his ego.

Paul can choose to appear…or not to appear in a photo when you take his picture. He can choose to only be seen as energy on film. When you take a photograph of him, according to how he chooses to appear in a snapshot, you may only get energy forms. A few other spacemen I met in Brazil also have this same capability. I've been in photos with Paul where my own body began to disappear because specialized energy extended from his body into my own auric field. It is hard to get a good picture of him in focus because he is so often in a different state of vibration than we might expect in ordinary human terms.

Although our naked eye doesn't see these energies, the camera can capture them, just as the tape recorder in voice tape phenomena records voices and sounds from other dimensions we don't ordinarily hear. In other words, these energies function in the sub-audible or super-audible ranges, giving us extended hearing, and wider vision in the ultra-violet and infra-red spectra. We see only within a very small range of a vastly greater visual scale. There are other octaves of vision. Clairvoyants, clairaudients and certain instruments record frequencies of seeing and hearing that have little to do with infra-red or ultra-violet. They are obviously registering sights and sounds perceived in the higher octaves of light and color, music and sound. People with ultra sensitive hearing may be clairaudient, that is, hearing broadcasts without radio; voices and music from the spheres.

These energy forms that appear are made up of elemental forces or spirits. For example, there are three types of fire. Electrical fire is the highest. The next one is solar fire. The third one is fire by friction, though we do have spontaneous combustion or chemical fire which comes under the classification of solar fire. All three fires function and operate as a result of fire electricity. Here, we can produce heat. In its highest aspect, it is electricity. Paul is likely operating in the solar realm, though we don't have instruments to measure this. I hope that science eventually develops more sensitive instruments, because we could learn much more about ourselves. There is a wonderful book called *Cosmic Fire* by Alice Bailey. If you are interested in this phenomenon, this book could change your philosophy, your life…

In a photograph of Doña Elza, standing alongside her husband Tite, one can see the arrow of energy coming down toward the top of their heads, where a tremendous force of this energy is attracted to them. It well may be electrical in nature, and not likely a beginning materialization of ectoplasm. The remaining photo area is washed out in the type of energy field which seems to cause this special kind of photographic phenomena.

One more thing…For lack of a more specific or appropriate term, I call these people "spacemen" or "spacewomen." They come from our planetary existence in many ways. Not all enter our world in UFOs or spacecraft of a physical kind, some are born here, or have, later on taken over a body—often a damaged one, quickly repairing it with unimaginable healing skills—after a soul has departed from a deceased human being. Later a new personality emerges in a person who now demonstrates marvelous powers. These are all incarnating souls coming from somewhere in space, hence the term Spaceman/woman.

PAUL LAUSSAC

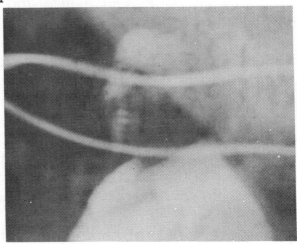

LOOPING ENERGY LINE…between Paul and camera.

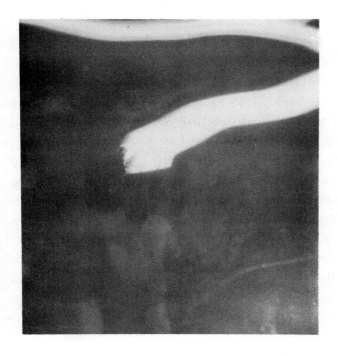

DOÑA ELIZA AND TITE…(lower left).

NEARLY ALL OF PAUL'S BODY IS MISS-ING… in this 35mm color photo. He seems to be able to create this phenomenon at will, if asked to do so beforehand.

Paranormal Power Knowledge is Coming Out of the Closet

An interesting phenomenon occurs with a pyramid. I've been publishing a newsletter for nine years called *The Pyramid Guide*, and I've been receiving letters from all over the world. People also come to see me.

Some California architects asked me to meet with them about six years ago during an outdoor conference at Pepperdine University in Malibu, California. They had erected an interlaced, rod framework of tetrahedrons which made up an impressive pyramid about thirty feet high with a nylon covering (see photo). We frequently get photographic phenomena with pyramid forms. I give workshops explaining pyramid energy and how to work with it. This is what we call "solarization." You can see in the photo that the subjects inside and outside are in different states of vibration. The body energy significantly alters the photographic result when the picture is taken of persons, animals and creatures inside.

In one picture of Paul, his body is not there. One can only see his head. When he was at my home in Santa Barbara, June 1981, we asked Paul if we could take his picture with a Polaroid camera, having him only show his face, so we went into the living room. I chose a spot and had Paul stand in front of the bookcase. He looked down for a moment. Then suddenly, looking up, said to our Brazilian-American friend, Mauro Pinheiro, who held the camera, "O.K." Mauro immediately snapped the photo. Presently, all that appeared was Paul's face. Still, one could clearly see the books on the bookshelves in the background, which should have been concealed from view by Paul's body. Mauro still has this photo, as far as I know.

Moreover, Paul doesn't go around saying, "Hey, look at me...See what I can do..." It isn't anything like that at all. He has other powers and exceptional healing abilities. As one observes Paul, it becomes patently evident that he can do things that are not considered normal according to orthodox scientific standards. He is not trying to seek glory or commercial advantage in any way because of his talents or extraordinary human capabilities. So, for these reasons and others, I trust Paul and accept the mind-stretching he has brought about in my life.

Paul, and other spacemen—at the risk of being ridiculed—are opening up to us; for today, these seemingly superhuman expressions will awaken in us our greater human potential. It is important that all who see any value in this discourse, please pass the word along. Eventually, as the number of aware and informed people increases, we will see wonderful things, discoveries now suppressed in science and psychology. Scientists too are beginning to come out of the closet, so we can move along more rapidly with natural—not just technological—human evolution.

REGULARLY REPORTED PYRAMID PHENOMENON...*the interior and immediate boundaries of Pyramid models often cause photographic anomalies and even electronic malfunctions in the cameras themselves. Here, we have a snapshot taken by Janek Kaliczak of Bambi Moise and George R. Madarasz, conversing inside of a California architect's portable pyramid structure mounted on the campus of Pepperdine College, in Malibu, California. "For some reason," says Madarasz, "a solarization effect seems to have taken place on the film—but the boundaries of the effect are restricted to the bodies only....If this had been due to defective film, or laboratory error, the entire frame would have exhibited solarization throughout and this is clearly not the case in this instance.*

Tomás Green Coutinho's Amazing Powers

Now I want to tell you a little about Tomás. His home is in Tres Corazónes, Brazil. I'm told he could levitate every chair in this room, even if they were nailed to the floor. I once saw Tomás pick up a fork between his thumb and index finger. It immediately folded double, broke in two, and fell in metal droplets on a table as if it had been melted in a 2000 degree furnace.

Tomás can transmute one substance into another. He can make coins out of buttons. He can take one of your buttons, and not only make a coin out of it, but you can tell him what kind of coin you want. At your discretion, you can ask for and receive (while you hold the button) a French coin with a date on it. On videocassette, I saw him transmute a $20.00 (Brazilian cruzeiros) bill into butter, and then transmute it back again. It was held by a Brazilian general, one of the country's leading metaphysical researchers. The bill—by the way—had the general's signature on it.

Tomás has many other powers as well. When one takes pictures of him, UFOs often appear in the background. These are not fuzzy images, rather one might see a clear picture of a mother ship and smaller scout-craft coming out of her belly. UFOs seem to follow him around. I'm not sure if these spaceships appear on film simply because Tomás wills it to be so, but from the photos I've seen, they are of excellent quality and of spectacular revelation. I now wish that I had asked him to bring forth specific elemental spirits—which he is obviously working with—and then captured them on film. Well, perhaps some other time...

Again, in the article I wrote for the *UFO Review*, "Spaceman Show Us Your Powers," you will find further details describing Tomás unusual powers and how he came to receive them in a near fatal accident.

Claims made by others for Tomás' extraordinary powers include the following:

That he welds metals together or separates fused metals with mind power alone; charges all types of batteries applying the same phenomenon power(s); transforms cotton into metal, and vice-versa; turns ashes into money, then enlarging or diminishing the object in size as he performs the mental act, and then turns the transmuted artifact back into its original state again, never touching the object, and achieving this feat while the specimen is even held in the hands of the astounded subject; and other unbelievable demonstrations.

I do have one other verified story to tell, related to me by Paul. One young man attending group meetings—where Tomás performed certain phenomenal acts at the request of those present—was told in no uncertain terms by his wife that she thought Tomás was just doing physical magic, with obvious deception. Her husband, saying this was not so, invited his wife to one of his meetings to see for herself.

The lady refused, saying, "If Tomás can truly bend metal with his mind, let him come here to our house, where I can control the conditions and stop the fakery."

The young man approached Tomás, explaining the dilemma and asked Tomás, would he come to their home to convince the doubting wife? Otherwise, the young man—to keep peace in the family—might not be able to attend the meetings any more...Tomás stood silent for a few moments, then suddenly thrust his outstretched right hand forward with a loud vocal "Hah!" "It's O.K. now," said Tomás, "don't worry, she won't give you any more agitation..."

Later, the young man drove home and walked to the back door of his house. There his wife stood in stony silence in the open portal, holding a twisted fork in her hand. "Come here," she commanded, "follow me." Then she led the young man on a tour through the house where open drawers revealed the presence of bent and twisted kitchenware and household utensils throughout the dwelling.

"That really made a believer out of her," he said. His wife even went along with him to meetings that were held later on; probably in hopes of getting Tomás to again straighten out the twisted tangle he so adroitly created, still removed by an outrageous distance of several miles.

Tomás could also sharpen dull cutlery with intense mind focus. The mid-thirty-year-old pharmacist was capable of unerringly driving an automobile on a winding mountain road while blindfolded. I was told that he could engage or disengage moving parts at will, without touching them. On one occasion, Tomás reportedly made a quick, right-hand maneuver with the steering wheel while in traffic (where there was no right place to go), yet the car continued on straight forward, as though the wheel had been held steady.

Finally, Tomás, who has been examined several times by Brazil's leading parapsychologists, and under strict laboratory conditions, was able to stage in one incident, a situation where he put an unoccupied passenger car through several highway maneuvers, solely starting, turning, braking and stopping the car with the power of his mind.

BILL COX (left) and Tomás Green Coutinho.

Japanese Youngsters Demonstrate Incredible Phenomena

The advanced 6th, root-race children in Japan, easily outdo our most celebrated psychics in the U.S.A., according to world travellers, Soichi Asai, President, and Hiroshi Ono, Vice President of the UFO and Parapsychology Researching Club of Kyoto University, Kyoto City, Japan, who visited the author in Los Angeles May 16, 1975.

"Uri Geller's earlier visit to Japan generated a large wave of psychic activity among Nipponese children," they said, "many actually upstaging Geller's most spectacular feats." Asai and Ono told me the known number of psychically active children in Japan, closely approached some thirty thousand in number.

At first, the children could only bend spoons, knives and other light utensils, but later on they began to demonstrate various new and unique psychic abilities, according to their own self discoveries. For example, here were a few phenomenal talents that came to light during the interview:

"Some youngsters found they could predict the type of order of playing cards dealt face down on a table," said Asai. "Others were able to mentally generate a thought photograph on camera film, exposed in total darkness." One child caused metal objects to disappear in local space. Psycho-Kinesis (P.K.) moving objects by mental direction soon became a rather common occurrence. "Teleportation, prophecy and telepathic, mental radio communication no longer remained unusual forms of expression in Japan," said Asai and Ono. One boy they knew could simultaneously see happenings in the present or shift into cognition of future events, merely by gazing into a water-filled washbowl. Another youth with P.K. abilities was able to recharge batteries by touching them.

Masters of esoteric teachings have long predicted the dawn of new root-race births which are presently occurring on a planetary scale. These children, advanced in their evolution, prove extra-sensory perception is not extra at all: It is *Extended* sensory perception.

The highly potent Atomic Energies unleashed by the Atomic Bombs on Hiroshima and Nagasaki, at the close of World War II, may have altered Japan's immediate environment, giving it new rates of vibration, thereby affecting the psychic capabilities of that nation's newborn children.

Some of the most dramatic "Psychic Photography" ever witnessed by the author, was shown live on national television a few years ago.

A Japanese youth mentally created a familiar building or landmark, held it in concentrated focus for a few moments, then in the manner of Tomás, released it with a forward thrust and loud "HAH!" Lo and behold, a reasonably clear image of the structure and surroundings then appeared on previously unexposed photographic film lying before him.

Although this phenomenon has been duplicated by Ted Serios and other adults during the past 100 years or more, the significant difference here was in the quality and consistency produced. The youth, Masuaki Kiyota, born April 10th, 1962, has an unusually aware sister, Kazuko, who is now 34 years old.

Masuaki feels he is aided by a spirit guide, known to him as Zenefu, who came to him in 1974, opening up the boys unusual psychic talents, which includes mentally bending spoons. During the year when Masuaki was born, and at the time of his birth, both of his parents saw strange lights, one above the child's head, and the mother being immobilized for a few hours at the time of the infant's birth, said she couldn't see Masuaki, at first, because his body was surrounded by a peculiar opaque, white mist.

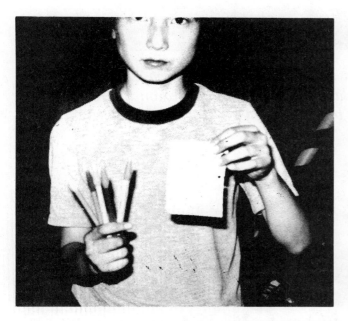

A UNIQUE KIND OF HIGHER MAGIC ... Akiv Haga, age 12, displays colored marking pens and note pad paper he uses during amazing psychic demonstration in Kyoto City, Japan. Akiv then throws capped pens and blank paper into the air ...

IMAGES, SENTENCES OR COLORED DRAWINGS created in Akiv's own mind suddenly appear on the sheet of paper as it returns to the ground. The mystery of his feat increases as the pen tops which are not visibly seen to move in the air, upon later inspection, are abruptly rearranged in a different order in matching or unmatching arrangement.

BENDING SPOONS with mental energy (P.K.), by Japanese children has almost become a national pastime since Uri Geller's visit to the Great Pacific Island.

TINY WATER SPIRIT...appears in unretouched photo. Gloria Ramsey of Gardena, California and her brother-in-law, were viewing the sea on the rocks at La Jolla, California, when this welcome but uninvited Nature Spirit loomed on film, lower right.

PHOTO ENLARGEMENT...reveals attitude of this little fellow, possibly a Water Sprite, who according to site reexamination and perspectives, cannot have been more than ten inches tall.

Mystery At Stonehenge

A correspondent, James Hamnett, of Great Britain, wrote as follows:

"Energy is form and form is energy. Unless one is aware of the production and management of this free energy in certain situations, unexpected events may occur.

"Tom Graves in his admirable book, *Needles of Stone*, writes of a friend's experiment that went wrong at Stonehenge in England. The young man was experimenting with an approximately two-foot high ankh-shaped wire aerial. He wondered if the ankh could pick up energy from the stone circle. It succeeded rather too well.

"Grave's friend had climbed on top of the roof of a car in the Stonehenge parking lot nearby and held the ankh by the loop. He pointed the open end away from his body and moved it around in a sweeping arc in the manner of a scanning radar aerial.

"The moment the ankh came into line with the Stonehenge monoliths, the young man felt a sudden and violent surge that seemed to burn his arm and he momentarily lost consciousness. When he regained his senses, he realized that he had been thrown bodily from the top of the car and his arm felt paralyzed.

"After six months, Grave's friend finally regained full use of the afflicted arm. For this reason, one shouldn't play around with these energies. There are too many unanswered questions regarding certain aspects of form (free)-energy at this time. The ancients and probably the Atlanteans knew about this higher energy and its uncontrolled manipulation. Rediscovery of these subtle but powerful energy forms and devices seems to have unfolded at an accelerated rate during the last two decades. Free energy may have a universal appeal in these times of energy shortages and curtailment, but a word of caution should be sufficient to the unwary experimenter."

What I'm interested in knowing: Could the automobile have acted as a cavity resonator, the ankh an electroactivator, and could the Stonehenge circle, having been erected upon a connecting nodal point of earth's magnetic vectors, produced the higher life energy current that threw the young man down from the rooftop?

THE ROD AND CHANT THAT CAUSED STONES TO FLOAT... Accounts of mind-controlled levitation often appear in mythological tales and legends of the ancients. Certain sounds issuing from drums, bells, cymbals and specially designed musical instruments may have sparked the levitative phenomenon. But even more so, the human voice singing the right tone or combination of tones might have done it.

The massive stone blocks in the Great Pyramid, the Colossi, Stonehenge, and world's megalithic structures may have been vibrated aloft through the cooperative chanting of hundreds of workmen, while the boulder's direction and movements though the air remained under the control of the wand-wielding high priest in charge.

Tibetan masters reportedly lifted rocks weighing some two tons. Through conscious direction of the will they presumably elevated ponderous stones to a ledge 250 meters high, while producing sounds from cleverly designed, wind instruments.

An ancient Sanskrit script seen in the Indian temple of Hoysalesvara reads: "Some day man will raise the bull and hitch the twelve wheels to the carriage which will obtain 2,000 elephants, strength in one strength, 10,000 horses, speed in one speed, and then man will be able to travel up to the sun."

Capturing Energy Forms on Camera

We know that in the world it is very hard to separate one category from another, except that certain mediums do produce ectoplasm from the ether, have the power of levitation, independent voice mediumship, etc. This doesn't necessarily have anything to do with what I'm describing here. We are considering the possibility of certain humans being in different states of vibration and the camera recording what we don't ordinarily see.

As space-persons intentionally or otherwise change vibration upward, their bodies begin to give out more and more light. This was told to me years ago by a clairvoyant in Vista, California, who has higher vision. There was a wonderful radiance in her countenance. She could see trees and creatures and people as light forms. It is sometimes difficult for her to see in detail what we ordinarily observe in the physical. An Indian Holy Man coming out of a meditation may occasionally have to squint his eyes to make out the features of the person before him because he too sees them as a light form. This is possible because his vision has become attuned to other planes of existence. The camera somehow captures this.

These are all regular photographs taken with standard 35mm color film. We have tried to work with infra-red with some minor successes, and with ultra-violet, we might also produce some surprises. But with just ordinary film, under ordinary circumstances, we're photographing entities from other dimensions. I'm not sure how they fit into the fifth kingdom, the angelic world, but they are beings who live in other systems, maybe coming from other planets, other planes of existence. Perhaps their world occupies the same space we do, yet being spheres totally unknown to us, unless they begin to appear in our photographs.

When pictures of a Los Angeles woman are taken, the same thing happens. She is usually in a very high state of vibration. When the photographer who took the pictures brought them to experts, they couldn't account for the anomalies, saying that "It is impossible for a high-speed 35mm film to produce such effects and colors." When he asked the experts what he should do with them, they told the photographer…"better than risking unpopularity…making waves…it's better to destroy the slides, and forget the entire matter."

These situations are not rare, unexplainable happenings in photographs. So, if we make a deeper analysis of the subject—with open, cooperative, expert assistance—photography's contribution to the so-called unknown will be of inestimable value. Unfortunately, several exceptional energy-form negatives and prints have been altered or destroyed in photo-lab darkrooms. Technicians are trained to see anything contributing to something less than a clear or near-perfect photo, as being caused by incompetent "shutterbugs," defective cameras or film, or unwanted reproduction "bugaboos." If you ever come up with an unusual photo, know your darkroom lab-man, and explain to him that you want the prints and negatives produced "as is" or you may well lose a once-in-a-lifetime photo opportunity.

Dowsing in Cooperation with Nature

Desired contact with the nature kingdom eventually brings rewarding experiences. Mushroom fairy-rings began to appear in my yard. It happened after I started doing nature photography, trying to communicate with life's unseen forces. This activity later led me to stop swatting flies and killing ants. When I finally could no longer kill any creature without expectation of just reprisal from nature, I started to have some visual perceptions and experiences. The aforementioned fairy-ring of mushrooms appeared in my front yard after a rainstorm. That was a nice gift because I know of people who have spent years looking for fairy-rings of even lesser quality in California forests.

EXPERIMENTAL DOWSING...with the aid of an open frame Pyramid and plum'bob type pendulum. The AURAMETER (in right hand) is used to detect changing energies from the Pyramid and pendulum.

There's a massive stone in Santa Barbara approximately 30' high on one side and 22' on the other. A fairly large rock grotto (carved by nature) will be found at the top, which will hold about 40 to 50 gallons of water. This is the place where (if you could see them) you would likely find water sprites, undines, gnomes and pixies, among other little earth spirits. Rock grottos often appear in what we call "Wild Gardens." Everyone who has a garden should have a Wild Garden Preserve, even if it's only a small patch in which nature can do its own thing without human interference. No human should ever tread into a Wild Garden. It is forbidden by these spirits for any human to go into these sacred sanctuaries.

I know of people who have unwittingly walked into these naturally wild and woolly places, later to become aware of an ominous presence, as though one were trespassing. I have on occasion blundered into Wild Gardens and had some unpleasant experiences. I now realize that if I had first mentally requested permission from the Landscape Deva, that is a Deva that is in charge of a specific vegetative area, and if I had received an O.K. through mental impression, the Deva's blessing would have saved me from unexpected events inside. Therefore, without such prior approval, there would be a certain element of risk involved. In California, for example, we have rattlesnakes, stinging insects, scratching cactus, poison ivy and prickly nettle weed all attracted to and loving the energies manifesting in Wild Garden areas.

If you'll allow the Wild Garden to have its due space in your yard, its presence will energize the rest of your planted and natural outdoor area. I've dowsed Wild Gardens all over the world. Some have later told me unusual stories characteristic of these capricious sanctuaries.

I've been locating underground water now for nearly fifteen years and was trained by a real master in this noble work. During the intervening years, since I began working with these spirits and great Devas, my percentage of success has substantially improved. This discovery has been consistent when I was confronted with difficult situations where one or more dry wells have been drilled or where there wasn't supposed to be any water at all. Here the client was finally asked for a dowsing survey only out of desperation, because geology and hydrology hadn't produced the desired result. Now I always attempt to make telepathic contact with the presiding Deva and cooperating nature spirits before beginning the work.

TOMATO PLANTS...and crops love Pyramid energy.

VOLUNTEER MUSHROOM Fairy Ring...in author's front yard.

Rosella Roberts photo.

ENERGY EMANATION…along the dog's undersides, probably in the process of materialization—the beginning of ectoplasm.

SOMETIMES A HALO SHOT…will produce a kind of photo solarization and bodily outlines which may appear as aura.

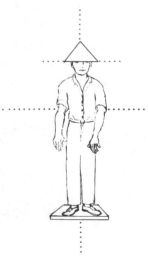

ILLUSTRATION…shows how energies emanate in focus from the body when a Pyramid is placed upon subject's head.

Dowsing Auric Emanations

When I first met Verne Cameron, I was cautious in acceptance, yet half wanting to believe him when he told me he could outline my aura.

I watched the old master bring the tip of his AURAMETER within a few inches of my body. The far end of the instrument leaned out as though pushed by a steady flow of air. Cameron didn't find much energy pushing out below my knee. I was relieved to hear this was not unusual.

As Cameron brought the AURAMETER upward, defining the auric outline from my arms, he encountered what he termed: "The more highly concentrated energy fields in the head and shoulder area." The dowsing device literally danced as the pointer passed my right temple. I asked him what happened. Without answering, the Master Locator, facing me, brought the AURAMETER up and parallel with the floor, and placed the tip alongside my right temple. The device bent sharply left, floating out and reaching a point about four feet from my head where it straightened into its normal forward position. As Cameron worked with the AURA-METER a few inches further out, it then bent back the other way in the direction of my right temple again.

Here, Cameron explained that this burst of energy was sending a telepathic beam. He also found a similar thrust from my left temple as expected. "But subjects measured usually produced the telepathic beam from one side or the other," he said. Cameron also delineated a twenty-two inch telepathic beam emanating forward from my left eye but no perceptive ray extending out from the right. This was to be expected, he said, as he'd never found an exception with hundreds of persons tested.

We ended the session with Cameron inscribing a thin, invisible, triangular shaped form projecting out from the back of my head. He labeled this ghost-ray the "telepathic receptor fin," and it was something over a foot long.

Feeling Emanations with the Aurameter

The late Verne L. Cameron's life-style frequently brought him to the threshold of the unseen. Once questioned about his unusual ability to "feel" mysterious concentrated beams from cones and pyramid replicas, he answered: "When the tip of my dowsing instrument first touches the energy field, it shoves off to one side or the other, like a concentrated squirt of water striking an inanimate object. I frequently lean the weight of the device against inertia (or its natural balance) and pull the tip up slowly alongside the suspected energy field. A soft, invisible, but deliberate action bends the tip away from the charged area."

"If I direct the AURAMETER's tip into the line of force quickly, there's a pronounced thrust—the radiations continue pressing it ever onward until the tip escapes to a point free from the area of influence, whereupon it breaks over, pointing back in attraction toward the origin of the etheric eddies," Cameron added.

"The AURAMETER's spring-poised tip enables one to respond to the higher vibrations through the touch of Dowsing."

Pyramid Replica Alters the Aura

Shortly before Verne Cameron made his transition into the beckoning planes beyond, we ran a little test with a twelve-inch square-based pyramid placed atop my head. We wanted to see if the miniature aluminum model of the Great Pyramid would alter the auric fields around my form. Cameron had previously found some astounding alterations in the human aura using cones and carbon magnets.

Before I donned the Pyramid, the Dowsing Master, with his AURAMETER, carefully traced the outer limits of my etheric outline. As expected, the energy field pushed outward from my figure about an inch and one-half in the region above my knees and on up along the arms to shoulder level on each side. A steady field of increased emanations in the head area pushed the AURAMETER's pointer out and away with a pronounced thrust.

Then, placing the replicap in position on my head, Cameron checked the earlier measurements. His determinations were as follows:

1. My ethic outline had entirely disappeared.
2. An apparently unknown shaft of energy poured outward from each elbow.
3. Cylindrical shaped beams raced upward from the apex above my head and downward below my feet. Verne, with the AURAMETER, found the lower rays going right through the seat of the chair I was standing on. The shafts darted outward, upward and downward, mysteriously suggesting a cross.

THE CAMERON AURAMETER…in action, formerly designed as an underground water locating Dowsing Compass, which later on, because of its extraordinary sensitivity, has been used to outline the human aura, form energies and remnant psychic vibrations.

41

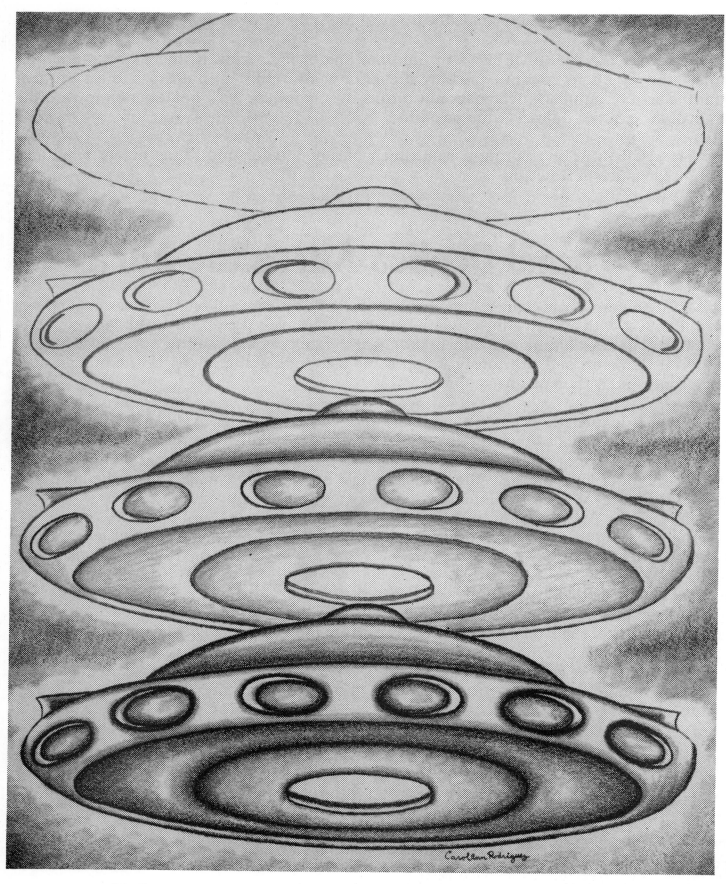

Materialization of UFO

Apparitions...Holographic Structures in the Sky

How can we explain the cause, effect and meaning of apparitions, ghosts, spirit forms and other nebulous phenomena? Ancient manuscripts and even contemporary history are replete with the sudden appearances, or visions of angels or God-like beings. The celestial visitor may often convey certain vocal messages to a chosen one. Prophecies occasionally follow in the name of the contactee. At other times, the visions remain silent and hover for prolonged periods of time before fading into oblivion.

If we admit the possibility of space visitors with technological skills far in advance of our own, three dimensional photography, holographic images created in mid-air can be the origin of apparitions. We can already view 3-dimensional images formed through ultrasonic means— a remarkable interchange between light and sound. Experiments now in progress also prove the human voice can be projected along a beam of concentrated laser light. With motion holography, we can also have moving, speaking constructions in space.

Apparitions seen in our atmosphere, along with other ghostly phenomena, including nature spirits, might just be holographic images created by masters, benevolent, higher intelligences from space and other dimensions. It seems their primary purpose is humanitarian and religious in nature and follows a certain pattern.

Consider the July 1917 Fatima apparitions in Portugal. The appearance of heavenly beings as a force was probably created to balance the negative, war-like consciousness permeating Europe before the close of World War I.

Note the sensational April, 1968 Zeitoun (near Cairo), Egypt apparitions. Warnings appear about man's hostility and greed, and insensitivity toward nature, earth and planetary life. The Zeitoun apparitions manifested in the warring regions of Egypt and the Holy Land. Then there were the astonishing apparitions over Korea a few years ago. Those who subscribe to this compassionate balancing of negative energies point out that the religious apparitions there contributed toward shortening the war of attrition in Korea at that time.

Some of the prophecies made after the Fatima sightings have been exceedingly accurate, with some yet expected to unfold.

Holographs are created with coherent light, waves running in parallel, as opposed to incoherent light emanating from incandescence, gas and flamelight. The 3-dimensional image also changes with the moving perspective of the observer. One can walk around the hologram and view it as a 3-dimensional object. Present laser holograms can attain several feet in size in each dimension.

From another point of focus, the photographic image produced by holography is nothing more than a thoughtform, frozen in time. If it is a kinetic hologram, then it is a thoughtform moving in space. The question is: Whose thoughtform? Our holographic science may now be catching up. But to what? Maybe some UFOs are holograms. Could the apparitions themselves be holograms projected from spacecraft?

Today's Thoughtgraphy, Tomorrow's Thought Viewer

Keeley

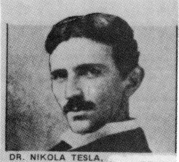

DR. NIKOLA TESLA.

THEORETICAL, CRYSTAL-LASER PYRAMID, THOUGHT-MACHINE... Nikola Tesla, in 1893, believed thought in motion could be captured on screen.

The late and vastly underrated electrical genius, Nikola Tesla, conceived the idea of thought-photography years ago.

"I became convinced," he told a reporter many years later, "that a definite image formed in thought must, by reflex action, produce a corresponding image on the retina of one's eye, and possibly be read by a suitable apparatus." Thoughtography, according to Tesla, was the basis for his system of television first revealed in 1893.

The master inventor planned to fabricate an artificial retina as a means of impressing thought signals on screen. He hoped to complete the broadcast by means of a simulated "optic nerve" and another retina at the point of reproduction. As Tesla conceived it, the two retinas would be multifaceted with checkerboard like patterns. "The so-called optic nerve," he added, "was merely a part of earth.

According to the report, Tesla had previously invented an instrument capable of simultaneously, and without interference, transmitting hundreds of thousands of individual impulses through the ground without the use of wires. He referred to a scanning device or cathodic ray, and reasoned that a thought or mental drama reflected on the retina could be captured through photography and projected on a screen. "Thus, the objects imagined or visualized by a person would be clearly reflected on the viewer as formed," he said. In this way the inventor believed all thought held in the mind of the test subject could be portrayed upon an optical surface. Scientists now studying thought-photography believe a crystal or system of crystals can be a clue.

"Crystals," they say, "are subject to mind-brain and energy patterns, and if grown to become specific geometric shapes, the prisms could likely be tuned to the mental frequency range of certain individuals," according to one spokesman. These far-seeing scientists foresee sensitive instruments containing numerous bands responsive to a multitude of thought patterns passing through crystals.

The Tesla-Scope for Interplanetary Contact

Nearly a century ago, when the idea of interplanetary communication was primarily a Jules Verne fantasy, Nikola Tesla was already performing serious research and formulating devices for the express purpose of contacting extraterrestrial "Beings." Tesla was the first man in our earth's history to record intelligently controlled signals from outer space. (See *Colliers Magazine*, "Talking With the Planets," February 9, 1901, "The Electrical Experimenter, April, 1919, and "Interplanetary Messages.") Tesla provided complete instructions for the construction of the Tesla-scope, which operates on the same principle as his anti-war device. The actual machine was put into operation by Arthur Matthews, of Quebec, Canada. Since it functions on the sophisticated, Tesla microwave system, it won't pick up conventional radio/T.V. broadcasts, but the instrument is specifically designed to receive transmissions from spaceships and can be equipped to receive from other planets.

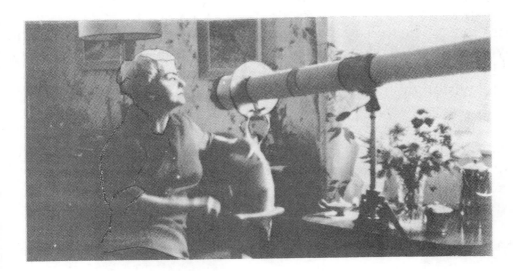

THE TESLA-SCOPE, AN INTERPLANETARY COMMUNICA-TIONS INSTRUMENT...*designed by Arthur Matthews, Canadian electrical engineer and built according to plans and notes conceived by Tesla.*

Pyramid, Voice-Tape Phenomena

A 12' x 12' base pyramid loaned to the late Bill Welch, of Encino, Calif. by *The Pyramid Guide*, has doubled the number of spirit voices registered on his reel-to-reel tape recorder. The results of Bill's tape experiments with tonal voice messages from the worlds beyond, again substantiates the pyramid's unique qualities in receiving and transmitting higher energies, higher octaves and harmonics.

William Addams Welch, former television and movie writer, was a most patient researcher. After a long period of testing, he was satisfied the pyramid, although not improving the sound level of reception, did appreciably step up the frequency of signals. Bill scientifically proved the authenticity of spirit-voice imprints appearing on unrecorded blanks winding through any commercially available recorder in a soundless room. "There was a definite drop in the quantity of messages when I removed the replica from atop the recorder," said Bill. "But after three months with the pyramid resting on top of my machine, the increase in signals continued, even after the replica had been removed."

For several years Welch had developed a remarkable collection of taped voices and a variety of chimes, bells and raps. They were usually preceded by a click, rap, breath or word cue, even after a decade of research, the unexpected occurred at every turn. For example, some messages transcribed at half, or double the midway speed of 3¾ forced him to increase or reduce the playback speed before it became intelligible.

THE LATE BILL WELCH...of Encino, Calif. holds Pyramid used in gathering sound from other dimensions.

Welch was even more perplexed in a tape experiment with two Arizona guests present. Eighteen outstanding tonal voice imprints of conversational quality impressed on tape, free of the usually expected static, whispers, tape hiss, inaudibles and other distortions. To his surprise, upon replay two days later, the voices were completely wiped out by some unknown cause. But curiously so, the ordinary external sounds of unexpected nature, such as traffic noise, a barking dog and shifting guests noted on the original playback still remained unerased and unaltered throughout the session. This suggests the possibility of the "other world" broadcast being transmitted on ultra high frequencies, beyond the range of reception by human ears and known electronic equipment's ability to reproduce once-evident audibles. Could the seemingly erased voices still be present on this tape, broadcasting in vibrations outside the range of human perception?

And if one has nagging doubts, consider the types of messages recorded from the so-called "other side." Advice in accurate form spoken by the voices came through about people Bill and his guests knew who had passed on. These communications were apparently initiated by skilled technicians living in a much higher state of vibration and intellectual development, far beyond our own here on earth. Their world allegedly lies in dimensions outside the etheric and astral planes interpenetrating and surrounding earth. "They have devised their own means of coming through" said Bill, "it's their test not mine" he explained. "There's little I could do that I wasn't already doing at my end. As they improved their techniques I began to get better reception. Sometimes they offered suggestions I could try, and we had our failures..." Bill could often hear these other world scientists discussing among themselves other means of approach, as though he was eavesdropping on a conversation filtering through a wall from a distant chamber.

For verification, Welch inquired in cross-correspondence through the old standby, automatic writing. The answers were often verified, as for example, with the sudden improved quality of reception when the Arizona couple was present. It showed how difficult it was to work within universal laws without a full understanding of their correct application," said Bill. "Progress has to be gradual. Yet, I've had some of this country's best mediums in here and there was no noticeable improvement in the quantity or quality of voice-tape contacts. So if this is a mediumistic phenomenon, where are we?"

Signals were often weak. Sometimes a single word required patient listening and interpretation. At other times, phrases, sentences and even whole paragraphs poured through. There were moments when atmospheric disturbance was stronger than the voices. (Experienced voice-tape researchers prefer night reception over daytime tuning.) Bill believed that a computerized filtering process might offer some solutions for clarity of listening.

Bill went on to explain..."These are very evolved people who at one time experienced life in the earth plane. They have had to lower the frequencies of their own bodies as much as possible to reach us, and it's no simple task," he added. "They want earth people to be comfortable with, and assured of the expectation of certain survival beyond physical death."

Great Pyramid and Replicas All Things to All People

The Great Pyramid can be compared with the sun. It is an instrument of life, power and the deeper mysteries.

Ask various members of a group: "What does the sun give you?" Answers will be diverse, yet correct. One replies: "The sun lights the world; it enables me to see." Another answers: "The sun warms me." Still another comments: "The sun makes things grow—you know—photosynthesis in plants, etc. The next exclaims: "The sun is a great electromagnet, without it there would be no electricity, magnetism, radio, global, or other energies." And finally: "The sun is the control key in our solar system, it keeps earth and our nearby planets in orbit."

Now, the Great Pyramid surely belongs in a category with the sun. Readers, writers, researchers, students, visitors, guests and travelers repeatedly tell us this greatest of all the world's seven wonders is an ancient "time capsule." Enclosed within its diverse stone blocks, passageways, chambers and measurements, in its precise location, orientation and outer structural form lies the key to the mysteries and wisdoms of the ages. It is, according to pyramidologists, a record of the history of mankind on this planet, containing exact information relating to the known and known (Biblical) past, a chronology of significant events encompassing the present, ancient prophecy and the future prospects of mankind's evolutionary growth or downward slide into technological oblivion and/or survival in the new age.

The Great Pyramid, and replicas, are alchemical instruments changing both organic matter (mummification, dehydration and preservation) and so-called inorganic matter (sharpening metals, affecting electronic devices, etc.) in beneficial ways. It energizes plants so they grow faster, better, attaining higher essence, *ad infinitum*…The Great Pyramid is a temple of meditation, initiation and rejuvenation. It is made up of two and a half million stone blocks. This great monument is a master slide-rule, computer, mathematical wonder.

AMATERASH PYRAMID, JENNER, CALIFORNIA

Forty-foot base side dwelling Pyramid, on a knoll overlooking the Pacific Ocean.

(Left) EXPERIMENTAL PYRAMID LABORATORY…designed and constructed by Dr. Ralph Sierra, of Puerto Rico, world authority and author of books on Bio-Magnetism.

Tachyons: Traveling Out of Time

Within the last ten years, science has discovered some mind-boggling things about the Tachyon (the Greek word for "swift").

First of all, the Tachyon can move faster than the speed of light, 186,000 miles per second, and suggests that time slows down when the light speed limit is approached. Secondly, this means that a paradox then occurs, for beyond the speed of light, the Tachyon can travel backward, as in Faustian Time; which says that when we travel slower than the speed of light, a clock will seemingly slow down; however, if one could move in space exceeding the velocity of light, the clock will appear to be running backwards.

Patient research and pondering reveals that the discovery of Tachyon energy presents disquieting scientific and philosophical questions. For example, a timed signal-using the world's finest Chronometers—could be received at a substantial distance before it was sent. Did it go the other way? Could Cause follow Effect in this instance? Strange...

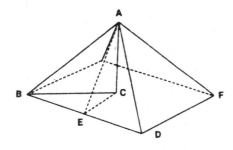

COMPUTERIZED FORMULAS FOR MAKING YOUR OWN PYRAMID REPLICAS

∠ CEA = 51 Degrees 51 Minutes 14.3 Seconds
∠ EAC = 38 Degrees 8 Minutes 45.69 Seconds
∠ DBA = 58 Degrees 17 Minutes 51.75 Seconds
∠ BAF = 96 Degrees 0 Minutes 19.987 Seconds
∠ CBA = 41 Degrees 59 Minutes 50. Seconds
∠ BAD = 63 Degrees 24 Minutes 16.49 Seconds
∠ BAC = 48 Degrees 0 Minutes 9.99 Seconds

DIMENSIONS TO ENABLE YOU TO CONSTRUCT PYRAMIDS OF ANY SIZE.

B-D BASE	B-A EDGE	C-A HEIGHT	A-E APEX TO CENTER OF BASE
1.000"	0.95146"	0.63661"	0.80949"
6"	5.70"	3.81"	4.84"
9"	8.56"	5.72"	7.28"
12"	11.41"	7.63"	9.71"
18"	17.12"	11.45"	14.57"
24"	22.83"	15.27"	19.42"
30"	28.54"	19.09"	24.28"
36"	34.25"	22.91"	29.14"
48"	45.67"	30.55"	38.85"
60"	57.08"	38.19"	48.56"
72"	68.50"	45.83"	58.28"
84"	79.92"	53.47"	67.99"
96"	91.34"	61.11"	77.71"
108"	102.75"	68.75"	87.42"
120"	114.17"	76.39"	97.13"
132"	125.59"	84.03"	106.85"
144"	137.02"	91.67"	116.56"
18'	17.12'	10.90'	13.86'
20'	19.02'	12.73'	16.18'
25'	23.78'	15.91'	20.23'
50'	47.57'	31.83'	40.47'

CALCULATED TO 10th

Example: Multiply the base times the edge measurement to find the correct size of your edge piece. When these 4 parts are brought from each corner to connect in the center or apex, they will automatically bring all angles into correct placement.

The Warp—Time In, Time Out

Time was…is…will be…Unaware, we alternately fly with, or resist time. We obey its imposing disciplines when we catch a plane. Time's inevitable march frequently awakens distress in some with a second look in the bathroom mirror. The typical American, obviously a victim of time, roots for victory at game's end, mentally fracturing the seconds with one eye on the clock.

By contrast, the Oriental waits patiently. It is in his nature to conserve and merge with time.

We perceive and comprehend earthly activity through our five senses by means of time. Literally speaking, time-sense, or lack of it, brings in, or takes us out of this world. When we are deeply engrossed in pleasurable activity, time really flies!

Time travel, where one moves forward or backward on a controlled wave of time, I believe, can occur within the higher planes of life, if a high intelligence so desires. Indeed it's a reasonable goal living in these strata of human existence. But consciously moving oneself, others, or things physically forward or backward in time…Ah!…that's another matter.

Consider "bi-location," where the mystic appears in human form at two distinct locations within a measured period of day. Again, to support the idea of time—perhaps non-time events—we have reports of "teleportation," the instant transference of material substances through solid matter outside the scope of known physical laws.

The late western mystic, Joel Goldsmith, and others, have described experiences of "instantaneity." Joel spoke of an incident where he, himself, and with passengers in an automobile, were transported immediately from a point on the Pasadena Arroyo Seco Parkway to central Culver City, California. The entire trip, according to Joel, consumed less than five minutes, a dubious feat attainable by any speeding race-car on deserted freeways.

Instantaneity apparently comes with more frequency to those living in four-dimensional consciousness, a state of being acquired through long periods of meditation and various physical-mental disciplines (the Pyramid form seemingly accelerates psychic energies associated with higher levels of awareness). Attainment follows repeated thought, desire, and emotion toward the higher state in that order, coupled with selfless dedication in its pursuit—but not always.

Regarding instantaneity, I once had a similar experience—not completely of this world. For years I've been seeking a logical explanation—in particular the first of three such happenings beginning in 1971. Later investigation revealed the surprising frequency of instantaneous occurrences encountered in others.

A lightning-like twenty minute auto trip on a Saturday night from Laguna Beach to Mira

Loma, California normally would have required at least forty-five minutes. At first, I thought my watch had stopped. It hadn't. I even considered the possibility of some monstrous joke, with someone conspiring at either end to set watches and clocks (including my own), ahead or behind, as the case may have been. But of course this wasn't so. I can only describe some of the latter part of the trip as lying outside the region of conscious memory.

It took more than two years of persistent study to partially find out the how and why of this strange episode living in and out of time. Instantaneity (as I later came to understand it) altered time during the brief excursion along the road—where I was suddenly vacuumed into a particular time frame, a warp as it were, where the normal progression of moments, past, present and future, all joined to become one unit.

Unlike cross-country "trance" driving, where one loses time-sense; then, later, in studying a road map, finds one has driven fifty miles further than realized—failing to recall, even, one or more small towns driven through enroute. And where one observes one's watch and dashboard clock registering the actual time lapsed…No, with instantaneity measured speed, travel distance and clock-time never jibe!

My body and transporting vehicle must have been momentarily propelled out of earth's ordinary succession of moments and into the timeless sphere of another dimension.

The Bermuda Triangle— A Time-Fold Pyramid

It has come to me through various intuitional, verbal and written means that the infamous Devil's Triangle in the Atlantic, off the coast of Florida, isn't the flat, two-dimensional triangle usually seen, as depicted in Photo 1. I believe it is a three-dimensional, three-sided pyramid (a tetrahedron), see Photo 2. I further doubt the possibility of it being a flat-topped three-dimensional triangular form as shown in Photo 3.

The mysterious pyramid form I refer to here is of course invisible. The fourth triangle—its theoretical base—underlies the three unseen, equilateral, triangular sides. All triangular frame measurements and base sides are of equal length, being approximately 1,125 miles long on any one edge. This interdimensional Pyramid stands above the mythical Bermuda Triangle area with its apex a towering 950 miles high above the Atlantic Ocean surface.

Within this gigantic, prephysical pyramid reportedly lurks a peculiarly sinister TESSERACT (an ever-moving cube in space). It is a three-dimensional space warp, navigating unpredictably within the greater pyramid form. This deadly time-dilating window above the sea in

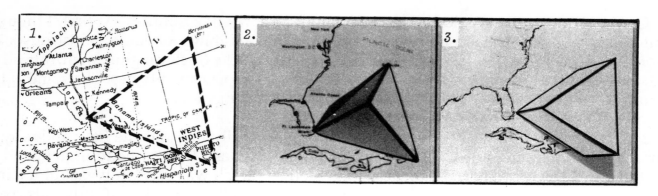

1. Bermuda Triangle   *3. Tetrahedron Superimposed*   *3. Overlying Flat-Top Form*

the triangle area is constantly changing its position, both in direction and altitude. The cube never leaves the confines of its incredible habitat—the great sea-sky tetrahedron. The Tesseract is allegedly a gateway to other planes, spheres and dimensions. UFOs apparently use these portals to enter and depart from our three-dimensional world. Once entry has been made by a person or thing through the Tesseract opening—voluntarily or otherwise—an immediate time change forward or backward occurs with respect to our calendar-clock-time dimension as we know it. This traveling cube within the great invisible maxi-pyramid has been clairvoyantly determined to measure approximately 30 meters along any one of its edges.

The first question to arise when the foregoing information came up during inquiry was: "How could a 425 foot-long freighter suddenly evaporate into a 117' by 117' rectangular time tunnel?" In later research with form energy, I found some possible answers: 1. The ship *could* be larger than the space warp. The immediate energy field surrounding the invisible Tesseract, or any form, is substantially greater in size than the basic form. 2. An expanded energy envelope maintains its pulsating field and identity in the manner of the human aura which is greater in size, being the matrix of one's physical body.

Tesseracts resemble in activity the so-called "black holes" in outer space. We have other Tesseracts within our earth-sphere, and these probably account for some of the sudden, "Now-you-see-them, now-you-don't" appearances and disappearances of extraterrestrial, alien craft reported in hundreds of UFO sightings since 1947. The larger and more powerful among these time-distorting portals will likely be found above our planet. Spacemen reportedly know where these intra- and interdimensional Tesseracts are located.

Besides the Bermuda Triangle, according to the late Ivan Sanderson, there are at least five other triangular-shaped Devil's Graveyards. These danger spots are located between latitudes 30° and 40°, both north and south of the equator. Lesser anomalies occur in another six such sites, making a total of twelve; with five found above and another five encountered below the equator. Each is evenly spaced 72° apart encircling the world. The remaining two magnetic space-time sites are found at the poles. A high incidence of human life, sea and aircraft losses have been recorded in these locales. The "Devil's Sea" northeast of Japan, though less traveled and not as well known, is even more nefarious in causing calamitous events.

Tesseracts of lesser size and intensity likely manifest as magnetic marvels at various planetary locations, such as the Gold Hill, Oregon Vortex and similar sites where these nodal points in the earth's magnetic fields appear. Earth's unmoving Tesseracts are somewhat deadened, being embedded and relatively fixed in the earth's crust. They seem to be responsible for a high rate of land-based accidents, though they are likened to energy medians (acupuncture points) in the human body. Thus the dangers of entering earthbound Tesseracts significantly differs from these prowling time-fold windows hovering within the invisible three-sided pyramids lying above land and sea.

A combined total of over 1,000 people, and 100 ships and aircraft have disappeared inside the Bermuda Triangle-Pyramid alone, without a single body or trace of wreckage being found. As mentioned, I'm convinced that the Bermuda Triangle's overhead structure in no way conforms to the five-sided, prism-like polygon shown in Photo 3, although it presents an alternative approach.

Nature spirits and other seemingly invisible entities can also use Tesseracts or space warps to lower their vibrations, thus attaining temporary physical expression.

THE SEARL LEVITY DISK…a man-made Flying Saucer awaiting liftoff, then aloft…

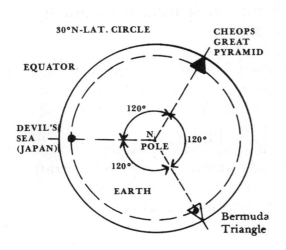

SIGNIFICANT PLANETARY POINTS…I first began to link UFOs with "Cheops" pyramids mentally when I noticed that the pyramid was on an angle exactly one half way between the ill-famed Bermuda Triangle and the similarly notorious Devil's Sea, off Japan. The two sea-zones seem to be haunted with excessive UFO activity, and a great number of aircraft and ships have disappeared there. The instrumentation in planes flying over the pyramid reportedly became inoperative and this seems to occur in the "Devil's Sea" and the Bermuda Triangle, and invariably when UFOs are near.
Contributed by Bill Whammond, Montreal, Quebec.

53

LONDON TO NEW ZEALAND IN HALF AN HOUR...Engineer John Searl, British inventor, has built some 41 flying saucers, all powered by an electromagnetic motor, reportedly capable of converting natural energy from the atmosphere.

The noiseless, population-free levity Disc requires no fuel and flies vertically when taking off and landing. An electromagnetic forcefield cushions the craft at supersonic speeds, according to Searl, who claims he has discovered four kinds of magnetism; whereas science only recognizes one type. Searl's Levity Discs vary in diameter from 0.9 to the manned spacecraft up to 11.5 meters across. One of Searl's anti-gravity discs has reportedly flown around the world several times prior to 1971...

ANTI-GRAVITY IS HERE...The Searl Levity Disk Generators, have developed from principles discovered in 1948. Ultra-high voltage electrostatic force fields are developed by segmented rings rotating in the disc's periphery. The craft's direction is controlled by varying voltage around the edge, producing unbelievable speed and agility.

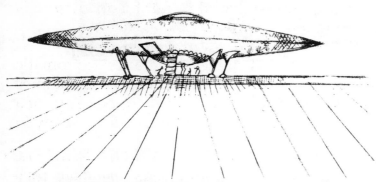

THE STARSHIP EZEKIEL...A rendering of J.R.R. Searl's 100 man antigravity, flying hotel and scientific laboratory. Seal envisioned construction of the craft beginning with "Project Impossible" in 1967 to "Possible," in 1968 but not with the size originally planned. He later defined the craft as "A city on legs." According to a February 1973 report, toys modeled after the magnetically powered spaceship were to be sold to raise funds to support the consortium's research and development work.

JOHN SEARL, *Inventor*

The Searl Levity Disk

John Searl, British engineer, was developing a generator for the Midlands Electricity Board in 1949. The device, consisting of magnetic rings rotating in different directions astounded the scientist by revolving with a sudden lift-off. The disk hovered overhead approximately 50 feet emanating a pink glow before racing off into space at incredible speeds.

In the ensuing years, John Searl and fellow researchers have spent over a million pounds, sending aloft some fifty levity disks. One ten foot diameter saucer, operating without fuel, reportedly crossed over Cornwall in a few minutes and went into orbit around the earth five times. A similar disk, traced by radio, traveled within a few miles of the moon.

Noiseless, high voltage generators surrounded by vacuum (magnetic thrust from centrifugal force) apparently collects solar energy and drives the craft without any signs of power pollution. The highly maneuverable Levity Disk seems to have unlimited speed and can easily take off or land with vertical movement.

The Searl National Space Consortium once made up of over one thousand shareholders and members throughout the world reportedly has tracking stations in Portugal and Denmark and an additional laboratory in Japan. To help raise money, the group was working in the mid-1970s on a two-man $66,000 show and demonstration disk, capable of taking off from England and visiting foreign lands. Observers below would see this disk as a ball of fire, presumably while pilots would be perfectly safe as high temperatures outside the craft couldn't penetrate the surrounding vacuum. Searl said, "The disk could reach the moon in less than an hour, and a trip to Mars would take about one month." Pilots could maneuver the craft by opening cells in the disk's surface altering the saucer's balance along the rim.

Some outstanding features of Searl's levity disk included fuelless operation, automatic beacon control, and the ability to hover, with its vacuum drawing and snuffing out the flames of forest fires. The disk might also be able to project this vacuuming capability into the eye of a hurricane to dissolve its force. "Moreover," Searl added, "the levity disk will operate easily in any kind of weather."

The consortium also plans to construct a thirty meter diameter, fifty-plus passenger disk with an additional 2,000 pound freight payload. But a giant 550 foot diameter levity disk, luxury hotel which could land for overnight visits at selected locations on the globe would allow tourists to sleep on board throughout their travels. This plan offered unheard travel accommodations, according to Searl and his supporters.

Even beyond, Searl envisioned *Starship Ezekiel*, a 1,000 passenger levity disk, which was in a highly developed planning stage, awaiting some $20,000,000 funding. This sky vessel would carry scientists in a matter of minutes to far off investigative sites not now accessible to them.

John Searl, lacking formal training in astrophysics, has demonstrated a profound knowledge in this field. His discovery of the phenomenon, prior to 1950, showed a spinning metal disk's magnetic force-field registers negative energy extending to the disk's periphery, where positive waves move inward to the craft's rotational axis.

Sharpening the Razor Blade with a Pyramid

Your pyramid replica may also be used in sharpening your electric razor. Allow extra time for mechanical shaving instruments, perhaps two days between shaves for best results.

The electric razor, when first sharpened under your pyramid model, may take several days charge in the initial sharpening test. Experiment by periodically placing your electric shaver in various positions and levels below the apex, for never less than a few days due to the variety of razors on the market. You may be surprised to find that an unorthodox mounting will produce the best results.

Place the head(s) so that the cutting edges face northward (never upward). Your electric razor may produce more satisfactory cutting power if it is not mounted on any platform at all but rather left resting on the base-surface inside of the replica. My triple-head Norelco, for example, sharpens best lying on its side with the cutting edges approximately aligned with celestial or magnetic north.

Place your "safety razor blade" flat on an eraser, square bottle, matchbox, or other small improvised platform, if you wish. To mount or not to mount your blade on a reflective surface is a matter of choice, and not a rule.

Set the blade with the ends preferably aligned in north and south directions. Allow several hours for the cutting edge to stabilize. Once the blade sharpens satisfactorily, replace it after each shave. Some say the blade "must" always be marked and positioned in the same manner; that is, the end facing north should never be allowed to point in a southerly direction as it may adversely affect its sharpening ability. No satisfactory evidence has ever been produced to show that this claim is valid, but since the mind of the operator is invariably involved, one might mentally program this limitation into the equipment.

Using the Pyramid to Preserve Perishables

University biologists claimed the mummified skin-cells of the ancient Egyptian Princess "Mene" were capable of life, even though she had been dead for thousands of years!

Colonel Richard Howard-Vyse, a century and a half ago, while exploring the Great Pyramid of Giza, came across a peculiar black powder covering the floor of Davidson's Chamber above the King's Chamber. The substance proved to be the mummified skins, shells, and exuviae of ancient insects. How, or when they got there is beyond reasonable conjecture.'

It appears evident the self-contained energy within the pyramids contributed substantially to the remarkable mummification techniques developed by the ancient Egyptians—methods unsurpassed even in modern times.

Dairy farms in Yugoslavia and Italy provide milk stored in pyramidal-shaped cartons. Reports are that this unrefrigerated milk stays fresh for prolonged periods of time.

A commercial enterprise in France preserves yogurt in specially designed containers. The same is done in Mexico.

Through the years, overwhelming evidence shows that a simple pyramid model, made of most any materials—as long as the construction is rigid and mathematically correct—will improve the taste of cheap wines, stale orange juice and retard decay and putrification in most organic, vegetative and already picked fruit; and even will cause accelerated growth in plants, crop-bearing orchards and gardens.

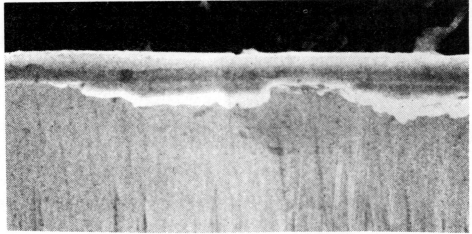

The cutting edge of this portion of a razor blade, magnified and photographed under an electron microscope, shows no appreciable change after use, even though the blade was substantially charged under a pyramid replica and continues to give a smooth shave up to 200 times.

Pyramids, Evidence of Higher Beings From Out of the Past

During several expeditions to Egypt, I soon learned that what Egyptologists and archaeologists tell us isn't always unquestionable fact. Unfortunately, their conclusions are based upon the examination of artifacts, dead bodies and bones; anything that can be materialistically verified. The more bones they find, the more they are convinced that Darwin was right; that we are descended from monkeys. If they want to make a monkey out of themselves, it's O.K. with me, but I think we are descended from wise forefathers, who evolved from even higher, more advanced civilizations, whose material records have been obscured throughout history. Prehistorical, antideluvian research is often difficult to verify because ancient technologies—unlike our modern, objective sciences—were of a subjective nature. Today we refer to this phenomenon as "Parascience."

Our technology is totally dependent upon our senses for verification. It so often denies the subjective aspect, the fact that we can often verify outer world data by going within. The method of dating is continually being revised. The idea that higher man just emerged four to five thousand years ago just isn't so. Some know it isn't so themselves, but few among these scientists are brave enough to admit it. One can find it frustrating going to an Egyptologist or archaeologist with what appears to be a startling new discovery. Because the materialistic scientist is locked in, if it is something that he must also weigh intuitively other than examining in orthodox scientific terms, his concrete mind usually rejects this information. Then again his colleagues might laugh at him. He wants to protect his position. So, there is actually a perpetrated fraud going on in science today. It is the scientific community that is resisting new knowledge. I've learned—as others have—to generally avoid the problem of unrealized expectations concerning physical scientists. We must go to the intuitive scientists, men and women who think and function on both inner and outer planes of experience.

Most humans are capable of contacting and cognizing other modes of intelligence. The gateway is found through one's intuition. The difference between the intellect and the intuition is that, whereas the intellect works with the parts, the intuition sees the whole. We could dismantle a brand new Ford and leave the parts on the shore of New Guinea, and the aborigines would use them as cooking utensils, weapons of warfare, or wear them as ornaments. Not having seen an automobile before, the pile of auto parts would be a wonder to them. We could go back there 10 years later, and we wouldn't see an assembled automobile on the shores of New Guinea. Some genius or informed person has to conceive or understand the nature of the whole, the complete unit. Being limited in scope, the intellect works with parts. It divides to understand. But the wisdom mind (intuition) unites to comprehend things. Understanding then comes from the union of intellect and intuition to conceive the "whole thing."

These ancient higher beings had this ability. When they looked at a work of art or a monument, they saw it in its totality. They were not linear in their thinking. An example of the process involved would be this: when one looks at the Sphinx, one might first see it as a religious

58

object if he were a priest. Perhaps it would be described as an engineering wonder, if one were to ask an engineer what he made of the ancient sculpture. Finally, one could look into the philosophy and legends surrounding it. We could eventually synthesize a dozen different processes.

The Sphinx is therefore not limited to one expression, nor is the great pyramid. This is why science finds the legends about the pyramids and the ancient Sacred Sciences hard to accept; because no matter what line of study one goes into, one could build a case for it. Since our technology is so linear, it is very difficult to accept the fact that in the past there were wise men within various races of people with the wisdom and intellect to create a monument or a work of art that was all-inclusive; one embracing the sciences of their time, including religion, philosophy and the anatomy of man. Their greater monuments, designed and constructed with near absolute purpose, remain for the most part, incomprehensible to the Western mind today. Scientific prejudice compounds the problem.

Curiously, we see and know only what we want to see and know. Humans have that strange gift to literally tune-out that which is too difficult to cope with or understand, retaining a blind spot regarding the information, until some future time when one can handle it. This phenomenon not only tricks one's mind but can blur the vision, dull one's senses and erase from memory valid and useful things concerned with life itself.

Multiple Perceptions

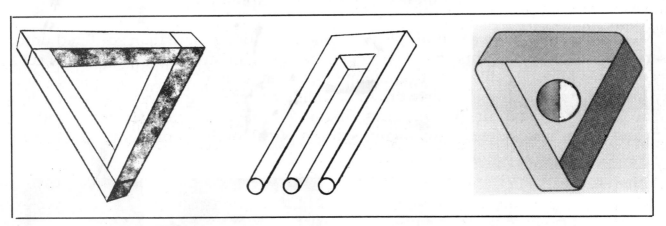

PERIODICALLY SHIFTING EYE DOMINANCE...from right to left, or vice versa reveals the strange phenomenon of impossible and mobius-type three dimensionally implied triangles and the illusory ghost prong of a fourth dimensional tuning fork (center). Hundreds of graphic optical illusions, presented to humankind—available at most local libraries—repeatedly verify that "seeing is not always believing." If such forms were seen airborne, how could one accurately describe the objects, let alone properly draw them to convince someone else as to what one might have seen?

Before me lies a chart of optical illusions. As my eyes shift from left to right eye dominance, a cleverly designed (two-dimensional) staircase ascends, seen as a left-side portal—now right—again left, and so on.

Another particular arrangement of geometric shapes (designed to trick the eyes) presents two rings surrounded by various patterns and colors. One unmistakably appears larger than the other, but I'm told the circles in the center are of equal dimension. I could compare sizes with a coin to make sure the author isn't trying to fool me, but I know better, his analysis is correct. This isn't the first time my visual apparatus has deceived me.

With some illusory patterns (Figures 1 and 2 shown), I cannot contemplate one in its entirety and full comprehend the design applying ordinary reasoning processes; the eyes insist upon focusing on some particular line, corner or section of it. After studying each particular geometrical form in its part making up the whole, I decide that all lines do lie in their proper perspective and am forced to admit: "optical illusion strikes again."

The Great Pyramid, Sphinx, Easter Island statues, Stonehenge and other spectacular world monoliths and megaliths, including ancient pictographs, petroglyphs, hieroglyphs, and symbols may at times also be likened to bonafide optical illusions; for we do not see them in their totality as combined scientific, artistic, religious natural wonders. We invariably try to comprehend them with the intellect which processes information by division, examining the complete structure according to a scientific, artistic, religious or engineering point of view, and then trying to take something of the whole out of its parts. The static mind becomes enraptured with the fragments of effects; the analytical mind proceeds from oneness to the wholistic imprint.

But how does one alter awareness in such a way that the entire design can be simultaneously understood in its totality? There are two powerful avenues of instant cognition available (among others) to any rational mind: Subliminal and Supraliminal Perception.

Meanwhile, one could say multiple perception is nothing more than scattered unfocussed observation. At one level, this would be a valid criticism, but in the higher planes of consciousness omniperception enables one to contemplate "what is" not "what only appears to be." We may have to study a structure, artwork or scientific object using a systems approach, that is, pursue its purpose and function in series, first in one way, then study it from another standpoint and so on. Then, after careful analysis, try to put all of the impressions together to hopefully understand its full content.

THE GREAT PYRAMID OF GIZA, EGYPT (Left)...A quasi-conical UFO, seen by thousands over Madrid, Spain in 1968 (center). Galaxy or UFO (right)? The stars and worlds of Andromeda closely resemble the compressed form particles of a UFO.

Thoughtform Device Powers Auto?

Reports from Europe claim a Frenchman has substantially increased his car's gas mileage using an imaginatively designed, crystal-mind generator. Some aspects of the story coincide with research information we have on hand in Southern California.

The unnamed experimenter, prompted by the kernel of truth so often found in legends and fables of the past, pondered the possible hidden meaning of word commands, such as: "Open Sesame!" or the secret order to elevate a magic carpet, or the command used by the young lady addressing the magic horse in "Beauty and the Beast" thus: "Go magnificent one! Go where I go!!!"

The young French researcher reasoned that a focused mind, capable of psychokinesis (moving objects at a distance with thought power) could emit a mental charge, a command through attention and intention which could be amplified by a suitable instrument and cause an action in, or upon a physical object or substance.

The Frenchman pored through ancient writings, ancient mythologies, religions, books on telepathy, metaphysical teachings, the general sciences and the mysteries of I Ching. He finally reasoned the "word" concentrated and verbalized as thought directed into a spherically enclosed crystal octahedron could be energized and amplified to produce a powerful result. He understood some principles of optics where certain crystal lenses could magnify visual waves, feeble signals in radio and other sound devices. Thus the young man acquired a lodestone shaped crystal, similar to two crystal pyramids joined base to base, and resembling the gold molecule, "the perfect metal." His mental generator (see photo), consisted of a glass, inorganic sphere, positioned upright at the base in an organic, wooden bowl. A cap at the top suspended a short string attached to the crystal surrounded by (organic) water. The completed thought-form generator was then mounted at approximate eye-level on the dash in front of the windshield of his sports car.

Since faith and unalterable conviction were essential for success he departed from home with sandwiches, dried fruit, sesame butter and apple juice. The car had a measured two gallons of petrol in the tank. He then issued the command: "Go Jahill! Take me where I wish to go!" The young man and his car "Jahill" headed for the countryside, unconcerned whether the gas tank supply would take him to any random destination or not, for he had food, good legs and confidence his mental generator would take him farther than ever before.

Previous tests indicated his car capable of 19 miles per gallon of gas during country trips. The route he now took was quite mountainous, adding further demands on the motor and gas mileage. After travelling 38 miles according to the odometer, the little auto advanced forward. The miles ticked off to 48, and at 50 miles distance he stopped the car, took a deep breath, sang a happy song and ran around outside for a while.

Again departing, he watched the mileage gauge register 60, 70, 80 and 83 miles where the auto came to a sputtering stop; all this distance on two gallons of gas. The mind generator worked, not even connected with the fuel or electrical system of his car. "Why did the auto stop?" he wondered? The Frenchman then thought of Wilhelm Reich's theory that the human organism can accumulate or disengage energy, and that this energy was capable of being utilized in mechanical tasks. Thus a motor driven with human (orgone-organic) life energy was a distinct possibility of enormous potential. "But another possibility exists," he thought. "The subconscious mind wills the event to occur—mind over matter. Mental consent can be given so mind and matter can function as one, their real and actual state."

In the past there have been reports of people running a car some distance after a gas gauge registered empty, its praying occupants eventually arriving at a service station. Was the automobile indeed running on fumes or did their combined mind energy enter into the phenomenon?

Kinds of Levitation

We already have anti-gravity in the world today (such as the Searle Levity Disk). Usual attempts to escape gravity in the past have been limited to the energy efforts of thrust, spin, velocity, and with various aerodynamic devices, such as lighter than air, gas-filled balloons, motor and jet driven airplanes, gliders and space travel rocketry. But there are other ways of inducing weightlessness. Humanly induced levitation, one of the most difficult to explain, gravity nullifying experiences seems to be most successfully achieved without intense, physical effort. This type of levitation, originating consciously or subconsciously in the mind isn't limited to the immediate locale, it can be achieved by the initiator at a distance, usually without props or devices of any kind.

There's no longer any doubt in my mind that mentally induced levitation of one sort or another continues to occur. I've personally witnessed, and have been involved in demonstrations of partial levitation. Table tipping and even horizontal levitation (psychokinesis), moving objects both laterally and vertically with mentally directed energy are in fact rather common occurrences. There are time-warping motions, physically created through accelerated bodily movements. By executing a kind of psychic-dance or using arm and hand gestures, it is possible to stimulate one's electromagnetic field, the human aura, as it were, summoned into action upon a physical object or substance.

Levitation of one's own body heads history's all-time list of perplexing, human uprisings. Mantras, deep breathing, deep trance and high emotional states, hysteria, ecstasy, and similar activities can apparently trigger the event. A sudden change of one's bodily vibration(s) explains to some degree what happens, but how or why self-induced levitation occurs without intent by some people still remains an incomprehensible enigma. Legends are filled with descriptions of ancient peoples who overcame the pull of gravity.

Did the Druids at Stonehenge of long ago truly master the use of the lodestone, golden arrow and fly over the land? Did long forgotten group rituals once induce magical flight? Druid magician, Abiris, presumably flew from Britain to Greece with the use of a golden arrow. Bladud, father of King Lear supposedly flew a huge craft, hewn and hollowed out of stone. Mog Ruith, Druid and Simon Magus reportedly mastered levitative techniques.

The elite among inhabitants of the legendary lost continents of Mu and Lemuria and Atlantis possibly knew the secrets of defying gravitation. We read of ships that rose above the waves during violent storms. Ancients in northern Venezuela reportedly fashioned small, delicate, stone pendants displaying bats and eagles, labeled *Kangplatten* (sound-discs) by German archeologists; discs, when struck at the proper pitch allegedly levitated the operator. Atlantean legends suggest rough-edged, ten-inch diameter, pure gold discs (one plate being ¼ inch thick and the other, a very thin disc), when struck together caused the wearer to rise above the ground. Another report says each child, upon reaching twelve, was given a personal, secret sounding tone, one that could be invoked to activate the instruments, followed by vibrational lift-off, and upsy-daisy. The mystical explanation for this phenomenon declares human beings to be the sum total of uncountable miniaturized, atomic universes; the atoms in one's body, once multiplied into action by one's conscious or subconscious will thus enable one to teleport upward, and outward through all space. One then overcomes all known physical laws, which are in turn superseded by higher, vibratory laws governed by the individual's consciousness.

In *Position Technic*, a book by Dr. Tim Binder D.C.N.D. (3704 Wonderland Hill, Boulder, Colorado 803020), Dr. Binder describes two case histories, previously recorded by Dr. C. Miles Martin, who originated the Position Technic method: 1. A woman who mastered posture was so well balanced in her motions that she activated the elusive levitative mechanism, and later learned to do it at will around the house. 2. Another male student of apparent ideal posture and bodily control found his feet reached earthly apogee some six inches above the ground while returning to the side of his waiting fiancee. Dr. Binder reports that he personally knew two men who had experienced levitation.

The Russian woman, Nelya Kulagina, recently levitated a small ball weighing some 50 grams before astonished scientists. This may only be the beginning of much greater levitative powers once possessed by our ancient ancestors. The elusive secret of levitation is likely embedded in the memory genes, latent within us all.

LEVITATION, SEEING AND NOT BELIEVING. The Match 1829 issue of Asiatic Monthly Journal *describes a yogi who could seemingly stay aloft without any visible means of support from twelve to forty minutes. The holy man readily repeated the performance anywhere without pay, not saying how he achieved the feat, merely that he had been accustomed to do so.*

Probing the World's Mystery Zones

We have scientific evidence—though limited in scope—of certain planetary regions and zones which are mysterious and defy rational explanation. I'm referring here to time warps, animal and mineral anomalies and distortion in vegetation.

Documented information is difficult to acquire in many cases, because scientists are generally reluctant to publish, or make publicly known, things outside the range of their ability to explain them. Reactionary scorn from scientific colleagues, regarding any attempt by credible investigators to rationalize hitherto unexplained events, is sufficient in itself to continue the ever-present addition of new links in the time-worn chain of scientific coverups.

At the present time, I'm working on the manuscript of a new book on Geomancy (GEO = Earth and MANCY = Divination of same, or Divining Earth–Sky Energies). In this study, I've collected a wealth of valuable research dealing with certain places on earth, which seem to at least temporarily suspend our accepted laws of physics.

Verified reports coming from responsible officials, bring to light the fact that humans are also affected by energy anomalies previously unrecognized or not understood by their nature.

In the early 1960s, the Schumann Resonance (ELF, extra low frequency waves) were discovered circulating in an envelope of energy close to, and surrounding, the surface of our planet. Because ELF frequencies as measured in cycles, closely match those of human beings, it became known that one's brainwaves could be entrained and even manipulated by a machine designed for this purpose. The Russians were discovered doing this to personnel in the American Embassy in Moscow. Russian covert activity manipulating ELF waves on an international scale has been exposed in the world press on a number of occasions.

Thus, if we are to believe reputable scientists who claim that energies, through nature or device, can somehow lock into brainwave patterns of humans, then the following series of seemingly unexplainable events may be explained as a function of, or aberration in the Schumann Resonance.

Within a straight stretch of Arizona desert highway, totally devoid of dips, curves, or other road hazards, a driver suddenly loses control of his vehicle and crashes on the roadside. Later, another car goes uncontrollably off the highway (in the same place) causing a fatal accident. Police investigation and reports by witnesses confirm that no other vehicle, pedestrian or creature was involved. The car veered off the highway at high speed. No logical explanation could be given for the crash in the police reports.

These ominous crossings apparently exist in other world locations, with essentially the same results. They function as earth energy bands (negative in their effect upon the awareness of humans) measuring from a few feet wide, up to widths calculated to reach a quarter of a mile or so across.

As far as I know, these "energy vectors," or "bands," can only be detected in three ways. 1. Through the acute sensitivity of one entering and passing its portal (which is energizing both earth and atmosphere directly below and above). 2. By Dowsing the site with a pendulum, rods or other Dowsing instrument, and, 3. By monitoring the changes in the brain wave activity of a human brought into these nefarious precincts. Other biofeedback equipment may or may not show change, so the Electroencephalograph (EEG) is perhaps the most reliable instrument available to date.

The cause of the aforementioned accidents may be described as a condition where the driver momentarily loses conscious awareness, similar to an operator who falls asleep at the wheel.

Approximately 300 kilometers southeast of Chihuahua City, and still further south of Jimenez City, in Mexico (near the northeastern border of the state of Durango), a region of strange proportions exists. Investigators have labeled the locale as "The Zone of Silence."

Intense night lights of unexplained origin, interrupted hertzian wave transmissions and strange plant mutations have been noted within the so-called "Silent Zone." On July 11, 1970, an Athena rocket launched from the White Sands, New Mexico missile range, seemingly selected a course of its own choosing, and was later discovered inside of a volcanic crater near the town of Cebollas, Durango, Mexico.

Shortly afterward, H. Augustus De la Pena, a metallurgic and chemical engineer studying the zone for possible oil deposits, found to his dismay that his radio receiver began to operate erratically. By changing location within the area, the radio would resume operation, or cease to function entirely causing interruption of any attempted transmission or reception.

A later scientific expedition to this mysterious domain, proved to others that De la Pena, wasn't exaggerating. Moreover, the investigative team reaffirmed De la Pena's earlier discovery that animal and plant life in the region displayed very different and peculiar markings, pigmentation and size in comparison with those seen in surrounding areas.

Black rocks with shiny surfaces labeled Guijolas, which were inevitably found on the ground—never buried within—containing various metallic substances, were presumed to be from outer space. Yet, there was never any sign that they had impacted into the ground, if they indeed fell from the sky. Numerous meteorites have been discovered in the Silent Zone.

One meteorite that fell on the Mexican town of Allende, February 8, 1960, surprisingly contained some of the oldest known matter ever to exist in our Galaxy. Another meteorite entering earth's atmosphere on a collision course with our Mariner Space Explorer, eventually went into orbit around our planet before falling to earth in the vicinity of the Zone of Silence. Another meteorite retrieved from this enigmatic tract, showed what appeared to be intelligently inscribed markings over its surface.

Scientific theories abound, but none really satisfy all components of the investigation.

Some include the assumption that these zones contain unusually large deposits of iron, causing magnetic anomalies such as those found at Gold Hill, Oregon, Santa Cruz, California, and other so affected world sites. Here photography shows that one can easily defy gravity, be seen to appear larger or smaller according to the position assumed by the person being photographed.

Regardless of the explanations offered, none of this satisfactorily explains the source of blinding lights observed in the night sky over the Silent Zone; lights that move both horizontally and vertically above the plain. Nor do other ideas offered by scientists yet satisfy the multiplicity of inquiries aroused by the world's numerous bands and zones of mystery.

The Disappearing Lake

Approximately 35 kilometers north of Belo Horizonte, in the state of Mirias Gerais, can be found one of Brazil's most incredible mystery zones; and there are many in that strange and often unfathomable land of UFOs and other enigmas.

Just bordering one side of Lagoa Sumidouri ("Disappearing Lake"), stands a 100 foot high, 1,200 foot long promontory. Now, the thing that makes this junction so extraordinary is the fact that the water disappears at this point on the lake, similar to the way water spirals down the bathtub drain.

Fortunately, the water inflow from tributaries on the other side, generally equals the water loss, so that during the wet cycles Lagoa Sumidouro's depth is fairly well stabilized. However, during dry periods, the lake literally disappears down the drain into the ever-thirsty orifice; hence the name Disappearing Lake.

No one seems to know for sure where the water goes cascading into the underground, but it is believed that enormous subterranean caverns underlying the promontory easily swallow up the lake's continual discharge, and provide a system of long distance conduits carrying the precious moisture to "God knows where!"

The lone hill, standing out above mildly undulating and surrounding flat surfaces, is an estimated 250 to 300 feet wide, where the lake water rushes down the sink hole. On the other side opposite, will be seen a shallow cave which apparently underlies the promontory, connecting with an almost undetectable opening near the sink-hole. Voices, and even whispers, from one side to the other, can easily be heard and understood. The cavity apparently acts as a sound or tonal amplifier. Loud voices or song may even hurt the ears of listeners on the opposite side.

In addition to these phenomena, the hilltop region lays claim to, and provides other unsolved mysteries, so many of prominence, that observers are forced to consider this area either blessed or cursed. Indeed, it is a site to be reckoned with, one which defies explanation in so many ways, beyond ordinary considerations. For example:

- During both day and night, UFOs are considered to be quite a common occurrence.

- Ancient Indian, or earlier race, pictographs can easily be viewed on the polished, vertical rock walls, rising abruptly above the perennially consuming drain pool. Towering cliffs on this, the lake-side of the promontory, actually incline off vertical, creating a precipitous slanting rock overhang. As one looks upward one soon feels the urge to move out from under this precarious shelter.

- My friend Hernani, who took Paul, Dona Elza and myself to the site, had on an earlier expedition, suffered bombardment from thrown or falling rocks. Hernani, and his companion, looking upward from a nearby sand pit projecting into the lake, both made out the movement of a white-clad, shadowy figure standing on a ledge, high-up near the summit. When they later climbed to the designated spot, there were no tracks, no signs of anyone pressing down the grass, no signs of loose rocks or any actual location above where their source could be found. Moreover, the falling rocks were wet, with no signs of water at the top.

- Huge trees project horizontally outward from the overhang, growing with profusion out of cracks in solid rock. How do they pull water into their root systems from such an inhospitable base?

- Huge niches, seemingly carved out of solid rock, nearly large enough to hold railroad cars, can be seen near the top of the hill. They follow verified lay lines, magnetic energy vectors running through the promontory. A Geomancer's delight.

There are several other head-scratching mysteries, but since space is limited, we'll just outline them for the time being.

For instance, giant bees, wasps (maribondes), butterflies and insects, huge beyond those known to exist elsewhere have reportedly been observed at Lagoa Sumidouri. In addition, the fish—at least some of them—are blind, indicating that they must occasionally swim upward and outward into the lake from the ever-dark caverns below. And finally, the local Indians, though they work the plantations around three sides of Lake Sumidouro, cling to the superstitions, and generally avoid the sink-hole and promontory. They and their forefathers have frightening memories of the place, which reminds one of a primal island jungle so often featured in movies about explorers and prehistoric monsters.

Paul Laussac, one of the "Walk-Ins" written about in this book, stands (far right) with friends looking out over Lagoa Sumidouri, the "Disappearing Lake."

Mysterious cliff where trees grow out of mountain at an angle and where early Indians drew strange disc-shaped craft on walls of caves.

Reversal of Gravity

Just about everywhere in Brazil you go you run into a mystery. Take for example the mysterious "fireballs" of Belo Horizonte which come up out of the ground.

Residents of this community have seen these strange objects for many years. According to the stories they tell, the fireballs are most often seen coming out of the base of a particularly large tree. When I was in Belo Horizonte on my last trip a man had actually gone to the trouble and expense of excavating the inside of the tree and had excavated enough room to put three or four railroad cars inside of it trying to find how far down in the earth these fireballs are coming from. No matter how deep they dug into the earth these fireballs still kept shooting up into the sky. They were not able to find the source of this strange activity. The fireballs seemed to come from very far within the earth, coming up into the sky, moving in an intelligent geometrical pattern, touching, doing dances with each other, as well as other impossible turns. They even changed color and size. Up until recently, these fireballs used to come out every night, but now they only come out occasionally.

As luck would have it, I was able to do my own research into the matter. Supposedly, there was a haunted house nearby that was three or four hundred years old, which has been reconstructed. Many residents believe there may have been spirits in that house which are responsible for all the fireball activity, but nobody can say for sure what is behind this phenomena. I did some dowsing at the house and was able to pick up an energy field and an entity which I could feel, but could not see. However, through psychic means, I was able to sense that the entity was a young girl who had lived in a neighboring house and had come to this house for comfort from her uncle. Before he died, he was able to communicate with her, which was a definite comfort because she was earthbound for so long, and is still earthbound, I believe. From what I could sense, she maintains her "pad" in this haunted house, in a small attic apartment. The fireballs come up out of the ground no more than 50 yards from this so-called haunted dwelling.

REVERSAL OF GRAVITY

Not far from the area where the mysterious fireballs have been seen is a region that is just as strange—if not more so.

On the outskirts of Belo Horizonte is a place that is called Peanut Hill—a bizarre locale indeed. If you pour a bucket of water on the pavement it will roll uphill. A bus takes tourists up there and the bus puts on its brakes and proceeds to roll uphill. If a person is walking or running downhill they have to accelerate in order to keep from coming to a stop.

Naturally, there is considerable speculation as to what causes this phenomena. I feel strongly that at this point there are many magnetic anomalies that are responsible for the reversal of gravity. There is an abundance of precious stones in this region, in particular quartz crystal which changes the frequency of the vibrations of the brain waves of the people that live in this area, giving them certain powers that we call occult. This also might explain why there are so many UFO contactees living near Belo Horizonte.

THE CAVE OF UFOS IN LAPA PINTADA

The area known as the "Painted Grotto" has to be among the most beautiful and breathtaking sights to be found anywhere on the face of this planet. Located at an elevation of 2,500 feet in the southeastern portion of the country, this grotto is responsible for much of the mining of precious and semi-precious stones done in Brazil. In the grotto is a cave with carvings on the walls that resemble UFOs.

I have been to this region several times, but the bulk of the researching going on here must be credited to Hernani Ebecken De Araujo who claims to have seen UFOs on four occasions, including the sighting of a cigar-shaped vehicle.

Hernani believes that the markings found inside the cave n the Painted Grotto were probably done by the local Indians recalling the visitation of ancient astronauts. Some time ago he went up to this cave along with several college professors whom he wanted to have verify his findings. To Hernani's way of thinking the drawings on the cavern walls were what we could call flying saucers. He says there is evidence of more than 50 saucers everywhere on the walls. From what he observed he also came to the conclusion that the Indians had a good notion of time and used a kind of clock which further indicated that they were very aware of the cosmos. Hernani says that there are other caves with similar drawings in which have been found many bones. He theorizes that the Indians went to these caves when they knew that they were about to die. Apparently, they had the capability to make dyes that lasted for hundreds of years. These people, he concluded, definitely were NOT savages.

Hernani tells this story of his initial visit to the Painted Grotto: "On the 18th of August, 1963, I visited the cave with the best drawings. It was the first time that any white man had ever been there. I found a message drawn by someone on a wall way back in the cave. The drawing had lasted about 11,500 years. In the drawing is a sun made from red paint. The sun is composed of ten circles and is surrounded by rays. Nearby are what appear to be two moons. One moon is in its first quarter. The other moon appears to be a "hollowed out" object of some sort. Located on the roof of the grotto directly overhead is a large cigar over one meter long. There is even a small saucer in the shape of a hat and a larger disc around 50 centimeters in size. The cave walls are covered with a strange form of language almost like hieroglyphics. This ancient language has survived all this time and is remarkable what it discloses. The message was to know the sun and the moon and the cigar and the saucer. There is another design which represents the key of time which appears in the form of a coiled serpent."

Hernani spent a lot of time trying to figure out what the second moon was. He researched two years in six different libraries before arriving at the conclusion that there must have existed an object in the sky that was hollow, and that this object came toward the earth, provoking an explosion caused by a supersonic impact. It devastated the axis of the earth and created the four seasons. This explosion supposedly also sank Atlantis and it created tidal waves. Hernani says that flying saucers come to earth from a space-time warp and that they may have put man on earth as well as the various species of animals and vegetables.

There is so much to see and do in Brazil as far as UFOs and other New Age subjects are concerned. It is a wonderful place to visit and I have had many fine adventures here.

TREE, SOURCE OF TWILIGHT FIREBALLS ...Strange lights, seemingly directed by intelligence, issue nightly from the base of this large tree in Belohorizonte, Minas Gerais, Brazil. The fireballs change in color, from red, through the spectrum into violet hues. They often move in vertical and horizontal lines, quickly changing direction and sometimes hovering above or near, but never touching onlookers. Efforts to find the firelight orbs' source by excavations at the base of the tree haven't solved the riddle: "They just keep on materializing from the lowest point in the ground," say witnesses. The gleaming spheres frequently ascend high into the sky, coming together in a kind of touch and kiss activity, often merging two fireballs into one. Dowsing the site at mid-day reveals a strong lifting motion with the Aurameter. Energy lines streaming upward from around the base cavity of the tree appear to move in a constant flow.

Thousands of years ago, UFOs paid a visit to the area known as the "Painted Grotto," where disc-shaped devices have been found on cavern walls.

Maybe Von Daniken Was Right!

Maybe he was right after all. Von Daniken says in his books on ancient astronauts that earth was visited thousands of years ago by beings from other worlds. Over the last few years Von Daniken has lost a lot of his credibility mainly due to his inability to substantiate some of his wilder claims. Yet you have to give the man credit, as he has managed to arouse interest in millions of previously unenlightened readers around the world.

In recent times, I've traveled many of the same roads as Von Daniken, and I dare say explored other puzzling sites he might not know about. These mysterious locations are spotted around the globe in remote areas of North America, South America and the Middle East. A number of these mystical sites have been pin-pointed as having been landing, launching and living pads utilized by travelers from space in ancient times.

What evidence is there that interplanetary voyagers arrived on earth eons ago? Such proof abounds in the seemingly imperishable records of antiquity in the form of monuments, great art works, incomprehensible symbols, ceremonial garments and trappings, architecture and anatomical pictographs. One stunning discovery I made is that a good percentage of the leaders and priests depicted have peculiar and unexplainable physical attributes.

Modern-day science has a way of explaining these physical anomalies such as six-fingered, six-toed beings. They say that they are flukes of nature, or if not an outright mistake, at least poetic license rendered by a prankish artist.

They have even said that the suppleness of limbs—where the feet of the supposed deities turn outward in a kind of ballet posture at 90 degree right angles from the normal forward stance—has been diagnosed as afflictions such as a club foot or bone cancer.

So far, I've run into these six fingered "humans" on the stone walls of Palenque in Mexico, in the ancient Amazon city of Akakor in Brazil, in Egypt and at other historical sites worldwide. This sixth finger in every case I've investigated was not a useless appendage of growth, but rather a functional limb in balance with the rest of the hand. At Palenque a medical doctor pointed out to me a stone upon which had been carved an entity with extra ribs. Similar clues have turned up at varied places; locations which are separated by thousands of miles of land and sea which supposedly the ancients would have not been able to cross.

Actually, it is easy for us to prove that various ancient cultures had absolutely no contact with other societies, even those existing nearby. It is, for example, an established fact that of the 52 tribes of American Indians living less than ten miles apart in the region around Alta, California, not one of them could understand each other's language.

In Karl Brugger's book *Chronicles of Akakor*, an Amazon Indian chief named Tatunca Nara claims he was led by a high priest into an underground city near the headquarters of the Amazon River far above Manaus in Brazil. Here, in a fabulous city built inside the earth, he was led to a vault which holds four blocks of transparent stone, something like glass or crystal. The Indian Chief says that within each block was the body of a humanoid laying in a pool of liquid. These beings were positively NOT of earthly origins, this being proven by the fact that each had six fingers on both hands.

Want additional proof? Well, did you know that in 1969 representatives of the National Indian Foundation flew over the newly constructed Trans-Amazon highway and discovered an Indian village populated by fair-skinned, blue-eyed, blond Indians?

Similarly, members of the same foundation encountered in 1971 yet another "white tribe" living on the banks of the Bacoia River. Some of these natives had red beards and long ear lobes, in the manner of Easter Island's historic "long ears." Two years later, further up the Ipuxana River, another blond haired tribe was found. Other reports of fair complexioned natives come from Brazil's Matto Gross, Peru and northern Bolivia. Finally, Quetezalcoatl, the legendary deity of Mexico and Central America may have been the same as the so-called god Kulkulcan, Itzamna (a Christ-like figure), Venezuela's "Xue," and Bochica in Colombia. All of these deities were fair skinned with blue eyes and blond hair.

SAMAIPATA is an unrecognized wonder of the world, located on a Bolivian mountain ridge. Deep carvings in the red sandstone cover several acres and challenge the most imaginative minds to come up with a rational explanation. The original works were completed far back in time. Weatherworn surfaces suggest it was done tens of thousands of years ago. Careful study reveals the fact that Samaipata was a

launching platform of immense size. Interconnected tubes, slots, apertures and tracks suggest that the total site served as a block on which a huge spacecraft must have rested. The site itself may have acted as a gigantic motor with the lattice work, channels and openings being the undercarriage block exhaust and intake conductors, valve and piston bores.

Notice in the center, two tracks one hundred feet long which may have been used as a downslope launching ramp. Explanations by archaeologists that these tracks were used as conveyors of blood in sacrificial rites doesn't satisfy the most gullible. With tracks of this size and length, what were they sacrificing—a regiment of King Kong-sized humans? Dowsing work done at the site reveals numerous energy vortices, a meeting of earth and sky energies. Moreover, Samaipata is the meeting place of great global ley (magnetic) lines that interconnect over the planet in a kind of geometrical grid system, and one that is reportedly attractive to UFOs.

Wonderful Discoveries in Egypt

It has long been known and prophesied that hidden key(s) opening little-known doors to the world's greater and lesser mysteries in Egypt would be found (one by one) sometime along the cusp of the Aquarian Age. People in ever-increasing numbers the world over feel an unfathomable compulsion, a peculiar magnetic pull or guidance, as it were, to learn and re-learn more about the enigma of the Great Pyramids and Sphinx. Such a group of inspired, inquisitive and well-informed researchers made the long journey to Cairo March 20th, 1979.

The research team included an Egyptologist, Pyramidologist, Educators, Writers, Psychics, Alternative Healers, Business Persons, a Photographer and supportive, aware investigators. Credit should be given to Mark Singer of Tulsa, Oklahoma, who organized the tour, who skillfully orchestrated the talents and personalities of some 22 investigators arriving from coast to coast, border to border throughout the United States.

All members of the expeditionary force looked forward with heightened expectations that some new and important discoveries would be made, and they were, as proven by our brief closure meeting, held on the plane during our return flight from Athens to the U.S.

No one really expected to be the "chosen one" who would roll back the great stone and open the bronze gate leading to the hidden hall of records. This was a reconnaissance mission involving perhaps a hundred or more individual and group tests. The homework had been thoroughly screened. Some researchers had proceeded nearly as far as they could go without further onsite investigation. A few others were making a return visit in order to verify previous information and to keep a watchful eye alert for new revelations.

The following reports represent only a small part of the trip's unfolding, to be highlighted by continuing research and awaiting publishing or copyright clearance:

Using a pitch pipe, I found that the King's Chamber, the truncated apex (invisible) chamber, subterranean compartments in the Great Pyramid, all beautifully resonating to the tone of middle "C," located at the center of any piano keyboard.

Two unexpected things happened during the several sound-chamber tests made: (1) An Egyptian guide leading a tour group into the King's Chamber from the antechamber called out: "Listen to my voice...It will ring out like a bell when I chant a certain note." I wasn't too surprised upon checking his intonation with the pitch-pipe. It was a crystal clear, highly resonating "C." (The humble guide had a strong masterful voice and apparently possessed the gift of absolute pitch.) His outcry caromed off the walls innumerable times, ever increasing in intensity, proving earlier reports by professional musicians and a sound engineer with sophisticated recording equipment that the King's Chamber in the Great Pyramid is a perfect sound chamber. It was, to be sure, purposefully designed and built as a part of a grand schematic make-up of the overall pyramid as one supernal musical instrument of cosmic proportions.

(2) Then atop the Great Pyramid at night, I again intoned the note "C" on my pitchpipe. (Other notes registered with surprising resonance but not nearly with the gusto of middle "C.") My personal guide who had made the climb uncountable times with tourists through the years, was also taken back by the startling resonance produced by the rather subdued tonal thrust of my tiny pitch pipe. He said he had never encountered this experience before. Both of us agreed the musical tone rang back as though there were invisible but very real walls enclosing the missing 33 vertical foot Pyrmidion. I had heard the neumonal, pre-physical capstone still rests up there atop the Great Pyramid (the secret chamber of the most High, the eye of God, symbolized on the U.S. Dollar bill). But this mini-apartment, lowered down to earth from heaven, reportedly cannot be viewed by the eyes of the profane, rather the presumed missing capstone has been there in its invisible state all the time, only beheld by adepts, certain masters and higher initiates who can see into this lofty vault and interpret the knowledge and wisdom of the ages believed encoded there. Can this towering secret pyrmidion be the long sought missing Hall of Records?

A NEWLY CONSTRUCTED PYRAMID...in the Weston Farell Shopping Center Complex, near Northampton, England. Photo courtesy of Nigel Pennick, editor, Journal of Geomancy, *142 Pheasant Rise, Bar Hill, Cambridge CB3 8SD Great Britain, who adds: "The British (driving) school of Motoring now has small pyramids mounted atop its cars."*

OUTSIDE THE GATE OF ROSETTA...where the momentous discovery by members in a group of 120 scholars and writers, accompanying Napoleon gave to the world the famous Rosetta stone. Found near the mouth of the Nile in 1798, the black, basalt slab provided with its Demotic and Greek inscriptions the major key and missing link in interpreting Egyptian hieroglyphics once considered undecipherable. The results, confirmed by Biblical archaeology, indicated that the Rosetta Stone's meaning alluded to a decree by the Egyptian priesthood assembled at Memphis, March 27, 195 B.C. honoring Ptolemy V Epiphanes (201–181 B.C.) and thereby enabling modern Egyptologists to regain knowledge of an ancient Egyptian tongue, long considered lost by earlier scholars.

Pyramid/Egyptian Mysteries: Unanswered Questions

After research expeditions to Egypt, Mexico and South America, one thing stands out above all other considerations: There's at least a partially organized coverup of vital information that would, if revealed, overturn many basic scientific beliefs about the origin of man. These disclosures would drastically contradict Darwin's theories on evolution. But even if revealed, and even if scientific information were suddenly to be made public, with the backing of orthodox scientists, it probably wouldn't be wholly believed anyway. It often takes generations to uproot very old and outdated concepts. Curiously so, in 1990, the flat earth people are still with us.

In attempting to untangle this strange web of mystery, one continually encounters the following barriers to investigation and verification:

Some of the most promising archaeological sites concealing the great mysteries have been kept secret by Archaeologists, Egyptologists, and Mayologists; in fact, declared off-limits to other than authorized personnel or carefully screened individuals and groups sympathetic with current and accepted scientific explanations; of those with money who support such projects and authorities with credentials from certain approved institutions. Independent investigators who usually function outside the perimeter of the foregoing elite, so often must scheme to find ways to probe deeper into things; to get often suppressed and overlooked "real facts." Then, when the something of value turns up, it is frequently ignored, immediately challenged or soon dismissed by scientific authority as "sheer nonsense."

Various puzzling artifacts, oracles and ancient trappings worn, held by, or surrounding priest kings, queens, initiates and the ancient magi as depicted in the historic pictographs, petroglyphs and stone statues are regularly explained away as only being symbols of life, truth, purity and so on; or are more often than not, disregarded in text and picture captions dealing with the subject.

Most all efforts to scientifically prove that the great pyramids and other massive stone structures were built with ropes, logs and hordes of driven slaves Hollywood style, simply cannot be verified by scientists who support those theories. The world's other great stone megaliths present another case in point.

Based upon the reasonable assumption that flash photography of ancient and fading wall paintings dissipates the quality of detail still evident in the ruins, why are serious researchers prohibited from photographing other ancient artifacts, ruins and certain equipment not so affected? Of course there are inconsiderate shutterbugs who can be annoying, or are the authorities in charge using these incidents as excuses to discourage the inevitable embarrassing questions that arise with photographic documentation? For example:

The Cairo, Egypt museum. The most significant discoveries concerning higher energy research cannot be photographed. One can only hurriedly make sketches. Descriptive captions identifying the subject or object are so often lacking in imagination. Mention is seldom made of their obvious mystical meanings. The museum catalog, along with these identification cards with exhibit number and usual textbook explanation leaves one hungering for something more than current offerings. New and proper ways of getting this precious information out must be found, uncovering and exposing the coverup to whatever degree it may exist.

Ancient Pyramids Ring the Planet

Recent discoveries of ocean-floor pyramids in the Atlantic support the theory that a belt of such land and sea structures encircle the globe. This "real in fact" pyramid meridian follows the 30 degrees north latitude arc girdling the earth. It is a notoriously active passage, intersecting some of the world's most significant land and sea borders and historic sites. This track also includes notable regions of magnetic anomalies: the Bermuda Triangle off Florida, the Devil's Sea south of Japan, and the Great Pyramid, that great time-capsule, observatory and library of stone in Egypt.

Knowledgeable researchers believe the larger pyramids of ancient times were likely prime sources of, and distributors of energy gathered from the Universe. Their secondary purpose applies in some measure current textbook theories showing the pyramids as only adapted to the culture, religious and burial practices of later civilization.

It now appears these pyramids, so defined on a world map or globe at the locations where first constructed will reveal *a secret message. The expected impartation* deals with the following observations: 1) The pyramid belt was constructed to reduce earth's wobble on its axis. 2) The spherical line of pyramids around the world were so designed as to channel higher energies for power and use in certain directions by the high priests and elite of prehistory civilizations. 3) The message also indicates that the pyramid meridian defines the best areas of search for the world's—as yet—undiscovered and most illuminating antiquities; the time is at hand in the Age of Aquarius, even though earth changes through the millennia have made deserts or ocean bottoms out of many verdant, populated areas along this belt. 4) The moment for New Age "tuning," a time for humankind to tune back into the very core of its inner being has arrived; a time for the human races to re-tune, back into one another, nature and the cosmos.

Excitement mounts as the eye follows the compass line on the world map, East or West of the Great Pyramid of Giza along 30° north latitude. Tracing the line eastward, we find Jerusalem nearby, Sakaka in northern Arabia, the historic city of Ur, Kuwait in southern Iraq, the seat of ancient Mesopotamia, the region of Babylonian, Assyrian and Sumerian peoples who constructed several pyramidal monuments and ziggurats.

This region of early Mesopotamia meets the junction of the historic, United Rivers, the Euphrates and Tigris waterways exiting as one in the Persian gulf near the latitude north 30° line. The pyramid belt continues on across the southern tip of Afghanistan and through Saharanpur, India. The Hindus, in their Puranhas, describe pyramids of such antiquity that they no longer exist, predating any known pyramids found on land today.

The eastern passage then proceeds through the northern tip of Nepal, and onward dividing the heartlines of Saka, Lhasa and Batang in Tibet. The world's highest, Mount Everest, lies slightly southward of the 30 degree meridian. Is it believed that Tibetan pyramids never attained the size of the "Cheops" pyramid. But they were distinguished by their multi-colored sides, inscribed with tribal symbols of deep meaning to the people who constructed them.

As mentioned in recent issues of the "Guide, the pyramid line advances eastward through China, not far south of the Shensi, Sian pyramids and Pan-P'O Village, pyramid complex. ChungKing and Shanghai are notably close to this circuitous, pyramid route. Continuing eastward across the Pacific Ocean, the world's ancient pyramid path advances below and lateral to the southern extremity of the Japanese mainland, north of, but very near to the triangular-shaped "Devil's Sea." The line then slices through a vast stretch of the open Pacific eastward and intruding into and beyond the northern tip of the legendary, sunken continent of "Mu." It was surely a land-base for two or more giant pyramids and countless, smaller step pyramids, possibly pre-dating all man-made pyramidal structures ever known. Midway Island, one of the last, visible landmarks of the ancient continent of "Mu" lies slightly south of the 30° north parallel.

Notice how the pyramid belt projects a line across the meeting of land and sea along the northern shore of the Gulf of Lower California, as it also projects across a similar plane in the Persian gulf, and continues this same characteristic in a line separating the U.S. mainland and the Gulf of Mexico—particularly at New Orleans. From there the pyramid meridian cuts across St. Augustine, Florida. Then it progresses onward through the notorious Bermuda Triangle south of the Bermuda Islands, where Dr. Ray Brown discovered his sea-bed pyramid and crystal. This is also the general area of the greater pyramids recently found on the ocean floor off Florida. Moreover, it lies within a portion of the suspected, lost continent of Atlantis and its sunken pyramids, perhaps the original site at the originating, master pyramid of the world's remaining pyramid structures found today.

From there, the belt literally runs across that vast, generally unoccupied expanse of the Atlantic Ocean to the Canary Islands; Ifni at Rio del Oro on the West Coast of Africa; Agadir, Morocco; thence to Beni Abbes, Algeria; to Gadames in Libya; onward across the southern tip of the Gulf of Sidra and back home to Cairo, Egypt and the Great Pyramid, navel of the world. A possible shift in the world's continents since ancient times may account for the Great Pyramid's present location at 29° 58' 51," less than one and one-half seconds variation from the actual 30 degree meridian.

Terry Allen of Los Angeles points out that the 30° parallels constitute the "Horse Latitudes." These dual line surrounding our globe north and south of the equator form the edges of the tradewind belts. The Horse Latitudes are noted for their calming, light variable winds, and were apparently fatal to horses transported on ships from continent to continent.

Does a pyramid belt then encircle the earth at 30 degrees south latitude? Information verifying this possibility has not been forthcoming. It's easier to establish another possible pyramid belt in the vicinity of the equator, as evidenced by pyramids found in Africa, Ceylon, Cambodia, Polynesia, and expected future findings in the southern tip of "Mu" in the Pacific. Mexico, Central and South America, mostly north of the equator have continuously revealed their large numbers of pyramids since the conquests of Cortez 450 years ago; but more on the equatorial pyramid regions later...

The Pendulum and The Pyramid

The pendulum responds above and around the pyramid or over the apex of a cone much as it reacts to a bar-magnet.

Recent tests by four individuals experienced in the use of the pendulum brought a unanimous opinion regarding the following results:

1. The pendulum self-activates its swing or swirl near and above the pyramid's apex, without any perceptible muscular influence.

2. The direction of the gyration—right or left—varies from one Dowser to the next, according to the pre-established code worked out in the operator's mind.

3. The pendulum readily responds to "yes" or "no" answers when moving above the replica's vertex.

4. The pendulum refuses to rest steady above the pyramid unless mentally directed to do so. Its natural tendency is to oscillate above or gyrate around the vertex.

5. As the pendulum gains rotary movement and is lowered, the arc of gyration widens without touching the replica—even down to the base.

6. A definite field of energy can be felt when lifting the pendulum up and along the ridges of the pyramid replica—more so than along the flat sides.

7. The main concentration of energy appears just above the pyramid's apex for some distance above.

Only the Sphinx Knows

THE SPHINX...reportedly carved out of natural, hard rock, was not sculptured at another location and brought to the Giza site as suggested by some writers on the subject. After careful investigation during two expeditions (March 1979 and again in the spring of 1980), it has definitely been determined that:

1. The Sphinx was indeed carved on site, likely from a stone hill, similar to, though much larger than the one seen in the Sphinx, profile backdrop (upper photo, next page). A closeup view of this stone hill, taken from a nearby cemetery (middle photo, next page), gives some indication of the type of natural structure and geologic material the workmen and artist's began with in shaping the overall Sphinx form.

2. Scientists from the University of California at Berkeley, have reportedly driven drill rods deep into the body of the Sphinx, apparently seeking hollow cavities and apparently without success.

3. On two occasions, other scientists drilled a number of approximately 4 inch diameter holes in the temple floor lying a short distance before the Sphinx's forepaws. In most cases, at approximately 30 feet depth, the holes began to fill with water. This discovery suggests that the old Nile River, which flowed past the Sphinx' forepaws thousands of years ago is still connected (at least to some degree) with subterranean water activity in the region of the Sphinx and Temple area.

4. To support the foregoing speculation, the following impartial evidence is offered: (A) A deep well shaft excavated centuries ago by hand, lying to the rear of the Sphinx, and on a line running in the general direction of, and between the Kephren and Cheops Pyramids, leads to ancient subterranean tomb chambers carved out of the Giza Plain's solid granite and limestone. Below the burial chambers the well shaft continues perhaps another 30 feet, where water is drawn out from above by an antique flywheel pump. (B) It's possible that this water source is derived in origin from Nile River seepage common to the shallow water veins running under and before the Sphinx, which is perhaps 70 feet in elevation below the Sphinx locale, then the supposed existence of a secret passageway in front of the Sphinx and the hidden temple presumed to be underneath, either do not exist, or are certainly flooded with water from the Nile which (by the way) now lies a few miles distant: The village of Nazlet El-Samman occupies some of the intervening distance, having been constructed atop Nile River alluvium laid down over the centuries with the ever changing and receding Nile River shoreline.

Finally, 5. Dowsing checks made throughout the Sphinx and temple complex area revealed (a) that there are water and rock/sand debris filled cavities at certain locations below the Sphinx locale. (b) However, no such cavities filled or otherwise existing could be found at the often suspected Sphinx forepaw region. Therefore, (c) the possibility of a secret entrance via the Sphinx forequarter area—one presumably leading to the presumed, secret Sphinx Temple and extended passageway, ostensibly running underground to and into the Great Pyramid—

could in part exist, if the point of origin can be found. Dowsing indicates that this legendary portal will more likely be discovered on a line running several yards northeast of the Sphinx, where it eventually follows a subterranean path leading in the direction of the Great Pyramid's southeast corner. In addition (d), further investigation should reveal the presence of heretofore unknown underground passageways and chambers below the Great Pyramid's northwest corner.

PROFILE OF THE SPHINX… looking east. This strange monument was originally carved out of natural rock onsite. Some masonry repairs were added later on. Note the natural formation rising up out of the Giza plain in the center background.

Spheres Falling From Space

Meteorites are ponderable, but symmetrically, near-perfect steel balls falling from the sky remains among the class of imponderables.

The "Fortean" mystery spheres, found from time to time throughout the world, seem to show mutual characteristics: 1. The ball produces magnetic and/or radioactive phenomena, and 2. Occasionally one appears to have a mind of its own, that is, rolling about and changing directions or starting and stopping, as though directed by some intelligence. 3. They range in size from eight to eighteen inches in diameter, and 4. are made of iron or unknown metals. 5. Footprints or other physical evidence has been lacking, suggesting that someone dropped the object at a particular site.

In the summer of 1972, a 16 inch diameter, 13¼ pound metal ball fell, burying itself 6 inches into the hard ground of a field near Ashburton, New Zealand. The walls of the two-part, carefully joined hollow sphere were a half-inch thick. Metallurgists haven't been able to identify the metal. The ball had a 6″ x 3″ gaping hole in its surface, as though ripped by explosives, or burned open by high-degree friction while speeding through the earth's atmosphere. The Royal New Zealand Air Force was called in to investigate and that is the last anyone has heard of the matter.

Then on March 27, 1974, Terry Matthews of Ft. Lauderdale, Florida discovered an amazing metal, seamless, stainless steel sphere lying in the middle of a field on Ft. George Island, owned by Antoine Betz. The object weighed 21¾ pounds.

The ball, labeled the "Betz space sphere" by writers, is proportionately equivalent to the earth's diameter 7,926 miles, the sphere being 7.96″ in diameter. Its circumference tallys 24.99″ corresponding to the earth's circumference of 24,868 miles. The strange magnetically charged ball attracts metal objects and voluntarily rolls uphill, but won't roll off the edge of a smooth surface. On one occasion the sphere rolled continuously for approximately twelve minutes. A one-eighth inch deep, triangular indentation scores its outer surface. The hollow sphere's magnetic features also include a north and south pole, and it may have two others, all distributed an even 90° apart. The object's magnetic properties vary in the manner of pyramid replicas. The orb is remarkably sensitive to musical tones, actually giving out a humming sound in sympathetic vibration as it resonates to the sound of a tuning fork or a carefully plucked guitar string.

X-rays reveal three moveable one-eight inch diameter balls and an irregular shaped, fourth object free-rolling inside. Their function hasn't yet been determined anymore than the origin and purpose of the sphere housing them. Was it a UFO?

Finally, on January 10th, 1977, William McCarthy, of Wakefield, New Hampshire, discovered a 16″ to 18″ hole in the ice covering the 150 foot long pond of his rural horse farm.

Early reports claimed a high level of radioactivity was detected according to witnesses who said the object crashed into the icy pond during the night. The mysterious black "thing"— viewed by witnesses through the hole in the ice—apparently sank into the muddy bottom. McCarthy's frozen pond curiously turned slushy in five degree temperatures. Officials later called in, denied the presence of radioactivity.

Huge stone balls up to seven feet in diameter or more have been encountered by travelers in Central and South America. The incredible weight and precision workmanship in their making, coupled with their actual purpose, as with metal space spheres, remains a complete enigma. "We know little about these things despite our great technological advances and software computer sciences," say researchers familiar with the spheres. Did ancient visitors from space leave a little of their "hardware" around?

In 1897, a newspaper reported that a spaceship crashed near Aurora, Texas. "The pilot was 'not of this world' and was presumably buried in the Aurora cemetery," the article added. A metal fragment found at the scene has been examined by a North Texas State physics professor. His analysis shows the metal content is 75% iron, and unlike iron, it is shiny and soft, and peculiarly non-magnetic. A ninety-one year old resident of Aurora still remembered the incident when interviewed. An interested group suggested they would like to have the spaceman's body exhumed for further verification.

On an unforgettable evening in July of 1972, Edward Lunguy craned his neck to watch a mysterious orange light pass directly over the Magic City Shopping Plaza where he was to meet his grandmother. When directly overhead, it was the size and shape of a Klick market sign. "Then the object began to move as though some invisible hand turned a switch to start a motor. It moved slowly, sluggishly, towards the other side of town. It was as though whatever force controlled that movement didn't seem to care who saw it— and it didn't seem to be in any hurry at all."

Suddenly, when it got over a water tower about two blocks away, the object exploded in a silent shower of sparks and disappeared. "It looked like the Fourth of July!" Lunguy stated. Later, the witness found a sizeable piece of "something" in his front yard which he believes may have been connected with the sighting. Scientists at NASA and Kent University admit they are stumped. The "Sphere From Space" has never been identified

Baffling Phenomenon of Clairaudience

The human hearing range is indeed limited, between 15 cycles and 20,000 cycles per second—a trifle higher for females and slightly lower for males. Men and women throughout recorded time have reportedly heard voices and music when others in their vicinity said they didn't hear anything at all. The former are called "Clairaudients."

Science now knows it's possible for some persons to hear sounds emitting beyond the lower or upper ends of the presumed human audio range, just as there are those who "see" lights, forms, colors and energy fields not ordinarily seen by homo sapiens. We call them clairvoyant. Both types of gifted persons apply what is properly termed "extended-sensory" perception (not "extra-sensory" perception). There's nothing "extra" about it when one perceives outside the limits of the human audio or visual spectrum.

Various animals can hear higher or lower sounds than men, and insects communicate with one another in frequencies even higher, often undetectable by our most modern scientific detection equipment. These mysterious sounds, music of the spheres, voices from spirit or whatever one wishes to call them, must depend upon some kind of higher electricity, radio and similar vibratory forces.

There are records of both men and women who seem to hear a particular radio station broadcast without benefit of a receiving radio. Some have even gone further, sharing the program heard in one's head by opening one's mouth with outpourings of orchestra, announcer or other station programming. Investigators have attributed this phenomenon to the radio-sensitive person's dental-work, electrical conducting silver fillings, gold inlays and so on.

But, there's another material which has evidently been overlooked...It is wax.

In two separate and unconnected incidents, students in my workshops said that when using bees-wax earplugs to shut out external noises to enhance sleep or concentration, that in each case, a subtle but evident voice and/or music was heard. Both believed the audio intrusion originated in some local radio broadcasting station.

After pondering the mystery, it suddenly occurred to me that the natural ear-wax which we consider to be such a nuisance, performs some kind of electrical-radio function essential to our hearing faculties. In its purest state, the natural wax-like secretion in the human ear may be a subtle electro-chemical requirement also necessary for the production of clairaudient (extended) hearing and other delicate sound vibrations. Further inquiry may well reveal that the honeycomb, the antenna of insects, bird feathers, human hair, and chemically active, waxy substances provide the broadcasting and receiving apparatus that makes clairaudience, telepathy and certain human and creature ultra-high vibratory experiences possible.

Living insects have entered the human ear and died, where the body eventually became surrounded by a hardened wax. Could this be the origin of the old saying (when one secretly knows) that "someone put a bug in one's ear."

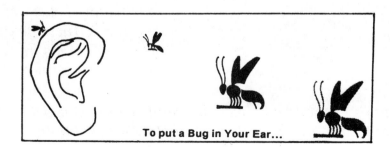

To put a Bug in Your Ear...

From time to time, elementals may take on almost human-like form such as in the case of this majestic Fire Spirit photographed at the precise moment of manifestation by Julia Burns.

Unicorn·Elf·Fairy

Thoughts Upon Knowing

These are those who *really* know. They often move in silence—
        Shall we know them?

Thus, we should be alert to their presence on any plane—
        And if possible know them.

And, there are those who *know they know*—
        Love them.

Moreover, to all who *share their knowing*—
        Bless them.

And also, with those who feel they know—
        Caress them.

And, with those who know they *don't know*, and say so—
        Trust them.

Watch for those who *meditate to know*—
        Encourage them.

But with those who *pretend to know*—
        Discourage them.

Furthermore, with those who *might know*—
        Test them.

And, when you meet those who *think they know*—
        Test them.

And, when you meet those who *think they know*—
        Listen! Observe with caution.

However, when confronted with those who think they know, but obviously *don't know*—
        Let your intuition be your guide.

And, further, with followers of the *lesser knowing*, or *unknowing*—
        Counsel when needed, without intrusion.

To go on, in meeting those who seemingly *may* or *may not* know—
        Learn from them according to your level.

Therefore when one flagrantly *doesn't know*—
        Be patient and quietly question this one's right to lead.

And finally, when you meet one who fears to know, or simply *refuses to know*—
        Give him or her your compassion.

For one day all who walk the Path will know what is worth knowing about a given thing—
though one should be suspicious of the "know-it-all." He knows even less than perhaps the
"know-nothing," who will eventually *know God.*

        And God knows all

Afterward

MASTERS FROM OTHER WORLDS...Did they come to earth from space in the long ago? Legends tell us of Venusians, Jovians from Ganymede (one of Jupiter's moons), and highly advanced and powerful strangers from Schwertz, site of a confederation of habitable planets supposedly located in the far outreaches of space.

Have extraterrestrial beings (currently referred to as Ancient Astronauts by some modern-day researchers) been visiting our planet throughout the eons past? Are they still around, their students, or at least their teachings? And what of the legendary masters reportedly living upon, or inside of this world? Do they truly exist? Do physical angelic messengers walk among us? A few knew how to tap the secrets of their presumed hidden portals, monasteries, secret initiatic chambers, mountain retreats, wisdom schools, or seemingly impregnable temples and subterranean halls of wisdom, would they reveal their secret and mysterious teachings to us? Maybe they are already doing so: angels appearing as humans unannounced...

Where can these masters be found, if they are with us? Are they able to move freely from the physical world into the non-physical as reported? Can they really achieve body invisibility and perform great wonders as described in writings down through the ages? Do white magicians truly exist? And what of the so-called black magicians, sinister members of the often-mentioned dark forces, sometimes referred to as members of the black lodge or "left hand path?" Are there such things? Or, is it all a grand invention stemming from humankind's unbridled imagination appearing in the records since the ancient days? Maybe it's all a product of humankind's unfulfilled desires, trying to find satisfaction through hero worship, blind relief in unerring, higher authority or a deep seated desire for protection from life's great trials.

In my travels throughout the world, testimonials persistently surface during private interviews, at lectures, workshops, seminars, conferences and the like. Input often comes unsolicited from varied, and at times surprising, sources: from mathematicians, teachers and advanced students in esoteric and metaphysical schools of thought, from closet scientists, from astrologers, astronomers, mediums, psychics and searching individuals in all lands. The subject of masters and adepts is occasionally pursued at New Age conferences.

Testimonials of personal, supernatural encounters are often made by individuals, and occasionally groups claiming to have received contact from, or having initiated dialogue with Superior Beings. Among them, some state that private instruction is being received from a higher source. These persons are sometimes referred to as mediums, mediators, messengers or contactees. One can easily find articles and photographs on this subject appearing in both new and old books, magazines and other forms of media. So-called marginal sciences and "lunatic fringe, claimants, purveyors of this presumed nonsense," are, according to orthodox science, "receiving more media exposure than they deserve." But this so-called nonsense has been going on for a long, long time. Some call it psychic phenomena, paranormal activity, parapsychology, parascience, the occult, metaphysics, spiritualism, esotericism and so on.

Years ago, while working as a newspaper reporter, I noticed the wide vision between totally objective, documentable writing and the subjective outlook. Just ask your local insurance adjuster how difficult it can be to arrive at the truth of an accident report. Confusion, outright lying, self-delusion, fears and other motives are ever at the root cause of conflicting witness reports. Seldom do all details furnished by witnesses and participants agree on fault and responsibility. Adjusters, lawyers and judges must often make crucial decisions based upon conflicting statements and testimony. In California, for example, we have what is called "the Last Chance Doctrine." Neither driver in the accident has to be 100% free of responsibility to collect damages in this situation. Nor is the "at fault" driver totally penalized, if it can be shown that the former—in the eyes of the judge or jury—contributed say 10% to the cause of the accident. Here the award is adjusted in favor of the least responsible driver on a percentage basis. So, witness reports and testimonials are, for the most part, subject to interpretation and the vagaries of belief systems held by others who make decisions based upon second-hand information.

Scientists might consider a portion of any library as fanciful, and though some research items here will surely test ordinary levels of logic, they are necessary to the whole study. It appears that there are two extremely divided lines of research going on in the world today: 1. The materialistic observer who mostly relies upon his/her senses to gather and quantify information. This method of investigation usually demands positive physical evidence easily discerned by one or more of the five senses in tests and/or observations which can be repeated numerous times. 2. The intuitive investigator who places a great deal of trust in his/her internal guidance, feelings and responses.

Both sides have their detractors, the close-minded unchangeables, tunnel-vision observers who must always be right, and self-deluded individuals with their head in the clouds, whose unproven claims we are supposed to believe merely because they say so. There are the "Chosen Ones," who loudly proclaim that only they possess certain secret information, channeled to them only from a higher source in the form of revelations. Their followers are only supposed to believe what they are told to know; these include individuals who depend upon someone else to do their knowing for them. But, as it often turns out, their leader may or may not himself/herself know for sure; for there are other leaders and teachers who, because of a monumental ego and other reasons known only to them, flatly refuse to admit that they cannot possibly know. We also have the "buck chasers," tall-tale inventors and rumor mongers who ever roam among us, skillfully seeking out the gullible follower with startling overstatements. These people quite often succeed in attracting followers, or at least believers, because these leaders apparently possess unusual personal magnetism, or a kind of spellbinding charisma.

Moreover, there's a small but ever-growing cadre of searchers who are ready to believe in almost anything if it's controversial, and in contrast, we have the critics and skeptics who are figuratively not prepared to believe in anything unless it's in a textbook, dictionary or encyclopedia.

For at least a decade, I have tried where possible to trace every lead and investigate the source. Fact or fiction, I checked details, interviewed principals, and synthesized any relevant information that might illuminate the mystery. Positive results have been produced by probing the depths of things considered mystical and paranormal, the spheres of the unknown.

Do I know any more than when I began the quest in 1968? This could be an embarrassing question, because after years of assiduous investigation there have been so many times during a search when I felt I knew less worth knowing than when the study first began. But as research continued, new things worthy of further study became known; things considered imponderable 10 years ago now seem rather commonplace. Well, that's evolution, or rather expansion. And so at this point in time, truly challenging questions once investigated now seem to have thoroughly justified the effort.

Nevertheless, one doesn't wish to waste one's time. It's better to move on to more satisfying pursuits than to be a victim of (self) deceptions. The thousands of hours of travel, researching in libraries, arranging interviews, attending lectures and so on, have been worth the effort in terms of the results thus obtained.

All 55 editions of the *Pyramid Guide* and most of my other writings have been made up of selected gleanings in this research. They are only a partial compendium of new and reinforcing knowledge now on hand concerning the mysteries. Nature and realms of the unknown at times will reluctantly give up their secrets. Despite its controversial nature, the information given in this book is offered in the spirit of truth, and I accept the responsibility which comes with added knowledge. Integrity must blend with the idea to know. The true way is ever straight. Its rewards are the joys of discovery and self-discovery.

Questions and Conclusions

Can we depend upon and believe the reports of others as to what they see, hear, decide, know, feel and claim?

Throughout recorded history we find uncounted testimonials and claims from persons who profess to know something which we seemingly should know. These persons who present this information can safely be divided into two classes: those who really know and those who really don't know, or those who depend mostly or solely upon their senses and those who rely more upon their feelings in receiving and processing information.

Somewhere in between, we see an expansion of a third type of investigator: the one who seeks a balance between the intellect and intuition, senses and feeling, knowledge and wisdom, which in their combined harmonious union produce understanding and a refined reality model specialized according to the life, needs and goals of the individuals concerned.

Physical-Prephysical Credibility

Is there such a thing...? To repeat: can we depend upon the reports of others as to what they s
hear, feel, they know, and what they claim?

1. If we can verify it too, with our own senses, then it must be so...
2. If we can't, because of inconvenience, unavailability of thing and method to be verified or if fc
some reason it's impractical, then we must trust those that have, or have had, this right or experience. Even though we haven't made a personal observation or had such an experience, we
then believe it, or not believe it in a second-hand way according to our conscience.
3. Can we be sure that the investigator, reporter, scientist or whoever is reporting accurately?
Sometimes there will be a dispute among so-called experts...interpretations often vary. New
information may later confirm or deny what was reported and believed earlier.

   Have you ever looked at distant galaxies and stars through the Palomar 200 inch tele-
scope? Neither have I. Yet we are expected to believe these scientists who have, and still do,
make reports of what they saw and most importantly how they interpret the information
received.

   Here, we're dealing solely with sensate, physical observation, the accepted orthodox, scientific approach to knowledge. Moreover, we usually have to wait for final analysis before the
reports are released. Then, some time later, an update is made, based upon newer information
and the report is changed, possibly negating previously known data.

   Thus 50, even 10-year-old astronomy books, except for useful photographs and some basic
information, are literally worthless today. They are being replaced by the latest in scientific discovery and reporting known as "Objective Research."
4. But today we have other types of observation pushing through for expression based upon
experience and a kind of inner knowing. These ways of gaining information are called intuitive
or subjective opinion by orthodox scientists. With few exceptions they will say that these
reports are—for the most part—not to be trusted, worthless, "sheer nonsense," and absolute
rubbish.
5. Here, the question arises: Can subjective information be trusted? Is it accurate, subject to the
same vagaries of change experienced by orthodox scientific reports? Has subjective observation held up through the years? Can we prove that intuitive information has been, or is of any
real value? Can it be quantified?
6. How do we sort out truth or fact from fanciful notion, self-delusion or even outright lying? The
best answer is to look to the source, the person or persons giving out the information. Will it
stand the test of objective analysis? Probably not right away. But from the standpoint of intuitive analysis it will, that is if the data is basically valid.
7. Problems with intuitive information are many because:

   a. It contains precognition, prophecy or altered time perception, past or future. How can anyone perceive out-of-world clock time? Here, one is immediately considered suspect in the eyes
of orthodox science.

   b. It relates to seeing, hearing, feeling or experiencing that which ordinary human senses do
not usually perceive. In these situations, one is invariably looked upon with suspicion. For how
can anyone see aura, spirits, read the akashia, have x-ray vision, clairaudience, etc. if other
humans among the masses don't? How can we know that they're really perceiving and reporting as they claim? Can they be certain? Do they tell the truth?

   One way to verify intuitive information is to see if there is agreement among other
so-gifted persons each unknown to the other. Is there basic or partial agreement? If
not, why?

PYRAMID KIT

The ancients were familiar with the power of the pyramid shape and how it could be used as an energy accumulator and to preserve. In recent years parapsychologists worldwide have tested the pyramid and found to their amazement that even miniature pyramids made to scale can produce some pretty astounding results when used under proper conditions.

The pyramid form on the inside back cover is of the proper dimensions to conduct such experiments on your own. It is not necessary to cut this book to use the pyramid. Simply trace the form exactly onto the sheet of ordinary paper and then paste it onto cardboard such as the type that comes with most men's dress shirts. Once you have done so you can begin to conduct your own experiments in the area of pyramid energy. Below are just a few of the experiments you can conduct in your spare time.

1. Researchers have shown that food tends to taste better when kept under a pyramid. Try some cheese, fresh vegetables, fruit, or anything else you normally enjoy and see if there is a difference.

2. Tests have shown that it's easy to reconstitute stale orange juice.

3 You can keep your razor blades sharp almost forever if you keep them under a pyramid. Try it with a new blade and see how long it will last compared to normal.

4. Pyramids have a positive effect on the temperature, making it possible to grow tomatoes and oranges even in the dead of winter while under pyramids. Even if you don't have a large enough pyramid to try such an experiment, try it out on a favorite flower in your yard and see if it doesn't last longer into the fall or even winter.

5. Investigators claim that if you put an old coin under a pyramid and leave it there for a month it will be restored to its original condition and a pile of rust will form nearby.

6. At least one individual who lives on the side of a mountain in California was having trouble with his TV reception, but when he used a metal pyramid as a TV antenna his reception improved one hundred percent.

7. For nine years the author of this book, Bill Cox, has been driving a car with a small pyramid mounted on the dash board and not only does he get extra miles to the gallon, but has never had any problems with the motor, nor does he have to change oil often.

8. Want to improve the taste of an inexpensive wine? Keep it under the pyramid for a few days and notice if there is a difference.

9. The yolk of an egg is said to take much longer to spoil if the egg is kept under a pyramid instead of being placed in the refrigerator.

10. Many researchers are convinced that the dunces cap or witches hat is based on the design of the pyramid, and that if you wear your pyramid on your head it may improve psychic ability or even cause you to feel more healthy. The next time you have a headache see if it doesn't take the pain away.

It has been noted, that in order for these experiences to work it is necessary to have a positive attitude towards these matters. Skeptics have poorer results than those who conduct such tests with an open mind.

Good luck in your own experimentation, and if possible the publishers would like to hear from others who have done research successfully with pyramids.

C ONSTRUCT YOUR OWN MAGICAL PYRAMID

Now you can construct your own magical pyramid and do the experiments on the previous page. You may either cut out this page or make a photo copy and then paste the pattern over a piece of shirt cardboard to make a pyramid that is sturdy and will stand up by itself. All you have to do is follow the simple directions below.

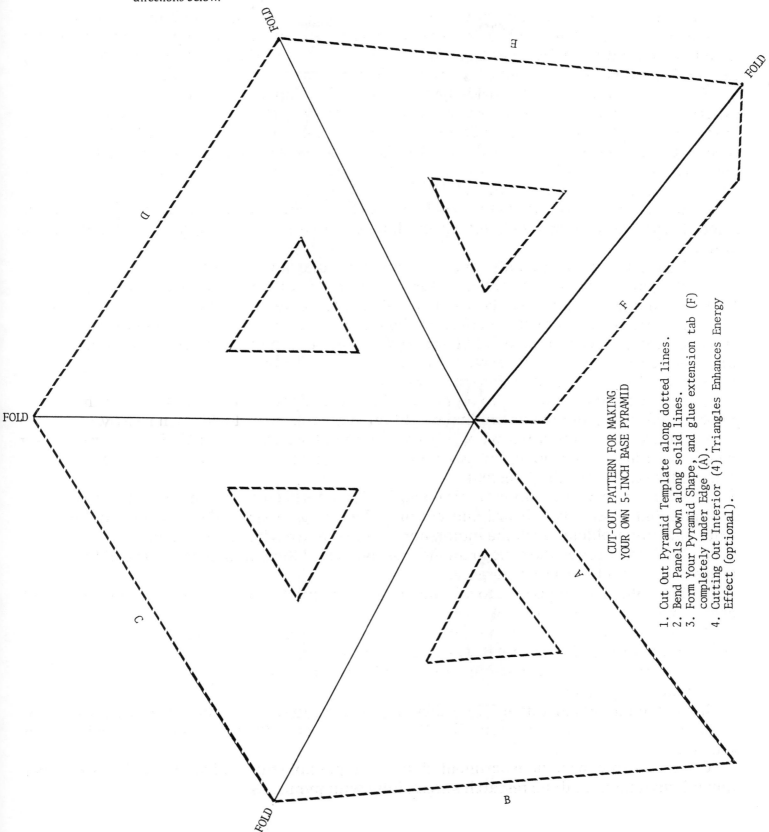

CUT-OUT PATTERN FOR MAKING
YOUR OWN 5-INCH BASE PYRAMID

1. Cut Out Pyramid Template along dotted lines.
2. Bend Panels Down along solid lines.
3. Form Your Pyramid Shape, and glue extension tab (F) completely under Edge (A).
4. Cutting Out Interior (4) Triangles Enhances Energy Effect (optional).

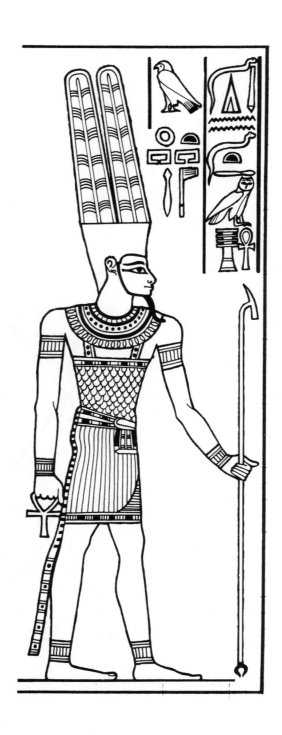